We Be Big

Other books by Rick Burgess and Bill "Bubba" Bussey

Rick and Bubba's Expert Guide to God, Country, Family . . . and Anything Else We Can Think Of

The Rick and Bubba Code

Rick and Bubba for President

Rick and Bubba's Guide to the Almost Nearly Perfect Marriage

Rick and Bubba's Big Honkin' Book of Huntin'

Rick and Bubba's Big Honkin' Book of Grub

Other books by Don Keith

The Forever Season

Wizard of the Wind

Final Bearing (with George Wallace)

In the Course of Duty

Final Patrol

The Bear: the Life and Times of Coach Paul "Bear" Bryant

The Last Christmas Ride / The Soldier's Ride / The Christmas Ride: Miracle of the Lights (as Jeffery Addison with Edie Hand)

The Ice Diaries (with Captain William Anderson)

War Beneath the Waves

We Be Big

The Mostly True Story of How Two Kids from Calhoun County,

Alabama, Became Rick and Bubba

by Rick Burgess and Bill "Bubba" Bussey

(with Don Keith)

THOMAS NELSON
Since 1798

NASHVILLE   DALLAS   MEXICO CITY   RIO DE JANEIRO

Published in Nashville, Tennessee, by Thomas Nelson. Thomas Nelson is a registered trademark of Thomas Nelson, Inc.

Thomas Nelson, Inc., titles may be purchased in bulk for educational, business, fund-raising, or sales promotional use. For information, please e-mail SpecialMarkets@ThomasNelson.com.

Unless otherwise noted, Scripture quotations are taken from the KING JAMES VERSION.

Published in association with the literary agency of Credo Communications, LLC, www.credo-communications.net

Scripture quotations marked NIV are from the HOLY BIBLE: NEW INTERNATIONAL VERSION®. © 1973, 1978, 1984 by International Bible Society. Used by permission of Zondervan Publishing House. All rights reserved.

Library of Congress Cataloging-in-Publication Data

Burgess, Rick.
    We be big : the mostly true story of how two kids from Calhoun County, Alabama, became Rick and Bubba / by Rick Burgess and Bill Bubba Bussey (with Don Keith).
        p. cm.
    ISBN 978-1-4016-0400-4
    1. Radio talk show hosts—United States—Biography. 2. Radio broadcasters—United States—Biography. 3. American wit and humor. I. Bussey, Bubba. II. Keith, Don, 1947– III. Title.
PN1991.4.R55A3 2011
791.4402'80922—dc22
[B]
2010038611

Printed in the United States of America

11 12 13 14 15 RRD 6 5 4 3 2 1

This book is dedicated to all the people whom God placed in our paths to enable us to become the *Rick and Bubba Show* and to all of you who took a chance on two students from Calhoun County, Alabama who didn't exactly sound like anything else on the radio. We are forever grateful for the doors God opened for us through all of you. Believe it or not, there are people in this business who actually believed and still believe in our show and this book is dedicated to all of you.

Contents

Prologue   ix

  1. The Light Goes On   1

  2. Radio in a Jug   13

  3. Too Good for Division II   29

  4. Grit and Wisdom   43

  5. "Hello, You're on the Air!"   51

  6. A Dark-Cloud Day   59

  7. "If You Had Come to Work for Us ..."   73

  8. Shakespeare's Worst Nightmare   83

  9. Fat Chat   91

10. "We're Test-Driving *You*!"   113

11. " ... Think of Us!"   119

12. Van Man, Errand Boy, and the Crazy Sign Man   133

13. God Is Great 147

14. The Eye That Does Not Blink 165

15. The Broadcast Plaza and Teleport 175

16. "Hey, You're Broadcasting!" 185

17. Satan's Miscalculation 193

18. God's Megaphone 201

19. Jesus, Take the Wheel 209

20. Who We Are 215

Acknowledgments 221

Prologue

"We've been test-driving you guys, and you are not the direction we want to take the station." With those dreadful words from the new management of our radio station, the world of Rick and Bubba took an unexpected downward turn.

By late 1998, the Lord had already blessed the *Rick and Bubba Show* mightily. He had opened doors—even though we had not always recognized them for what they were—and He put us in the right place at the right time. The show had miraculously come together and was prospering. Even though we were broadcasting from a station in Gadsden, Alabama, we had developed a strong following in the much bigger market of Birmingham and had begun syndicating the show to other cities.

Then things got even better. The station was sold and the new owners announced they were going to move the signal and studios into Birmingham. We were certain God was blessing us again and, based on the acceptance of the show already, we assumed that we were going to make the move with the station.

People had taken to our loud and rowdy brand of humor, mostly based on things that really happened to "the two sexiest fat men alive" and to our families, to people on the show, and to our listeners. Whatever else it was, the *Rick and Bubba Show* was real. If it happened in our own lives, it found its way onto the air the next morning. It was not like anything else on the radio, and that was a good thing.

It had not occurred to either of us that God had a plan for us, that He wanted to use our show for more than simply entertaining folks and selling things for our advertisers. If we had known that, what happened next might have been a whole lot easier on our nerves.

The new owners didn't sugarcoat it when they broke the news to us. Rick and Bubba were not part of their big plans for the station after the move. Our show—featuring two guys who didn't have deejay voices and who made fun of broadcast consultants, research-loving program directors, and boring radio—would not work in a larger, more sophisticated market.

They told us we could remain on the air until they replaced us with big-market personalities and a tightly formatted morning show. Then they would find us a station in Gadsden or somewhere else we could continue doing our little program.

That meant we were lame ducks for several months. Yes, we could have phoned it in. Or we could have tried to adapt to their format, doing celebrity birthdays and reading horoscopes and playing the songs that fit the format. Since we first started, however, the show had been about being real. Without even thinking about it, we kept it that way, but with no mention of the turmoil going on around us.

With all the uncertainty, there were mornings when we didn't necessarily feel like being funny. We didn't know which day's show might be our last. We had no idea where our next job would be. On top of that, we both had families to support and mortgages to pay. And besides, we were really fond of eating! We knew our show could continue to grow and prosper from the larger base, but now we were faced with the real possibility that we wouldn't have the chance to prove it to everyone else.

All we could do was keep on doing what we knew would work, even if there was no promotion, no backing, no guarantee that we would even be on the air the next day.

We know now that God was preparing us for something important. He was about to hand us a big old megaphone and trust us to use it for His glory. The last few weeks of 1998 would be an uncertain time for us, but there would be some other shows coming that would be much more difficult to get through. *The Rick and Bubba Show* has always been about the real things that happened to us.

What happened to us would not always be funny or easy to talk about. But it would give us the opportunity to touch more people more deeply than we could have ever imagined.

1 The Light Goes On

The alarm clock goes off at 4:30 a.m. at the Burgess house.
I—Rick—hit the snooze. The alarm is a Bose clock radio
because Paul Harvey, one of the greatest radio personalities
of all time, said Bose was the best there was. Like most
right-thinking Americans, I believe everything Paul Harvey
said. I almost always sleep through one snooze cycle, and
then I finally, reluctantly, crawl out of bed at 4:40. That is
not because I am lazy or lack a strong work ethic. The rea-
soning is that my rest is far more important than being
early for work. The way I look at it, there is no point in my
getting to the studio early if I am too tired to perform at a
peak level when I do get there. So long as I'm at work at six
o'clock with my finger on the trigger, the opening music for

the *Rick and Bubba Show* ready to fire off, then all is good. At least, that's what I tell folks.

Truth is, even though I've been getting up early to do a radio show for a long, long time now, I am not what someone might call "a morning person." The fact is that I maintain I earn every penny they pay me just for getting both feet on the floor every morning before the sun comes up. Everything else they get out of me after that—the show, books, public speaking—is gravy. Remember, though, gravy is very important to me.

I love what I do for a living. It was my dream from before I can remember. I just wish I could do it at two in the afternoon, when the sun is warm and the roosters have hushed.

There are plenty of mornings when, if I could reach my deer rifle, I would probably bag me a 12-point Bose alarm clock radio!

———

When we were growing up, my sister, brother, and I never had a doubt that our parents loved us unconditionally. They didn't have to tell us a bunch of times a day just to make sure we got the message. They showed unconditional love in everything they did, and that couldn't have been easy at times. Not when you consider some of the episodes I required them to look past.

My mom, Geynell, was a typical stay-at-home mother, first to us two boys—my younger brother, Greg, and me—and much later to our sister, Angey, who came along a decade after I did. And when I think of what we put Mom through and how she handled it all, I know she will be at the front of the line for sainthood. My dad, Bill, was a football coach. People have an image of what it must have been like growing up with a hard-driving, character-building, sell-out-for-the-team coach for a parent. But you know, hard-nosed and demanding as he was on the practice field, he was no Great Santini–type when he came home to his family at night. Bless him, he kept his job as a gung-

My 5th birthday party, Birmingham, Alabama

ho football coach and being a father completely separate.

That even worked out the same way when I later played football for him. I was not Coach Burgess's son when I was out there on the practice field. I was just another player and had it no tougher or easier than anybody else on the team. We were all equally miserable.

And Dad and I rarely talked over the dinner table about that day's practice or the previous night's game. What happened on the field or in the locker room stayed there, not all mixed up with a platter of biscuits and a dish of fried pork chops. That couldn't have been easy for him! I bet there were plenty of times he wanted to fuss about me getting myself blocked out of a key play or missing a tackle or dogging it on the end-of-practice wind sprints, but he simply buttered a biscuit and talked about something else.

When I was born, Dad was working as an assistant football coach at Woodlawn High School in Birmingham, Alabama. He was a key member of the staff of legendary coach Shorty White, who regularly took his team, the Colonels, to the top of the city high school standings. Coach White later went on to work for Paul "Bear" Bryant at the University of Alabama, and Dad moved up to take over the Colonels.

Dad made very little money, but he worked hard, doing something he loved to do, and that fact did not escape me, even at a young age. He taught class all day and coached football after school—usually until it got too dark to see the ball—and then coached games at night and watched film on weekends. He certainly taught me the value of doing for a living what you are passionate about, even if there are not necessarily many financial rewards attached to that package.

Dad got his first big break in 1971 when Oxford High School in East Alabama noticed the success he was having over there in the big city and gave him a call. They wanted to see if he was interested in making a move to Oxford, a small town very similar to Mayberry on the *Andy Griffith Show*, about halfway between Birmingham and Atlanta. The area was growing, the school was getting bigger, and the administration and parents decided they wanted to build up their athletic program to be more competitive. They made Dad the handsome offer of fourteen thousand dollars a year (which would be a sizable raise), and that was attractive enough to get his attention. But then they also offered him the position of athletic director. As both head football coach and AD, he would no longer be required to teach classes. He couldn't turn that down, even if it meant uprooting and moving his family halfway across the state, leaving a big town and going to a much smaller one and, in effect, building an athletic program from scratch.

So when I was six years old, we made the move east, out of the big city to a small house in a nice, calm neighborhood. I doubt the residents there knew exactly what a wild bunch had just moved in down the street.

Our new home had a covered carport, a big backyard, and a thick plot of woods nearby. That carport, the yard, and those woods morphed into our football field, battleground, racetrack, strange planets beyond the known solar system, basketball court, circus tent, church house, movie set, rock-and-roll stage, radio studio, and much, much more—anything our active imaginations could conjure up. My brother, Greg, and all the neighborhood kids became teammates, big-game hunters, fellow space travelers, animal trainers, movie extras, race car drivers, congregation, band members—whatever personnel I needed to fill out the cast of that day's gargantuan production.

You can see I was afflicted from an early age with the insane desire to be in show business in some way. I don't know where that serious genetic malfunction came from. Understand, too, that my definition of "show business" was extremely broad from the very beginning.

It could be sports, music, radio, TV, preaching, singing, playing guitar—anything to get me on a stage in front of people. And Lord help me, I had to be the one who was up front, at the microphone, carrying the ball, making the quarterback sack, always the center of attraction. If I believed in psychiatry, I might speculate that this unnaturally

5

powerful force was just my somehow seeking the approval or attention that I was not getting enough of at home. But that wouldn't be true. I lacked for neither approval nor attention.

That need to perform was just there, and I could not deny it. There is no real explanation for it. Old Rick just liked what he liked. And he liked him a ton of it!

We put on some of the most spectacular shows you would ever hope to see there in that carport in Cheaha Acres. It might be the Burgess High-Flying Circus, with our beagle puppies subbing as lions and tigers and us doing death-defying feats on the jungle gym. There were puppet shows there, too, scripted and complete with props and sound effects. We built vast amusement parks in the pine thicket nearby—"Frontier Land" with swinging-grapevine rides, "real" cowboy-and-Indian fights, and even more elaborate attractions designed to amaze and enlighten visitors.

First baseball team, the Blue Caps (no fancy uniforms). I am 7 years old.

The funny thing is that we didn't put those shows on just for the praise or the glory. Or even for the fun of it. No, we charged admission.

Parents, neighbors, other kids, aunts, uncles, everybody. No free passes to the Burgess High-Flying Circus or to Cheaha Acres Frontier Land! I was downright entrepreneurial about these things. It may

6

have only been a penny or a nickel for a ticket, but there were no unpaid admissions.

Even at that age, I realized two things: when you do a show, you put on the best show you can; and if you do that, you get paid for it.

That included sports. From the first, I figured "sports" was equal to "entertainment." When we had neighborhood football games, we had to have uniforms and coaches' shirts for everybody who participated. The "field" may have been a patch of Bermuda grass between our house and the neighbor's, but the yard lines were marked off as best we could do it. There may have been some misuse of Mom's White Lily flour on occasion, but if so, I'm sure the statute of limitations has run out on that. At least I hope so, or Mom may still take a belt to my behind. Those of you from the South know exactly how traumatic that can be!

Later on, when I figured out how to do it, I rigged up a cassette tape recorder and found a microphone that worked. One of the kids who was reluctant about getting trampled by us big 'uns would record play-by-play commentary, just to make it feel a little bit more like it was Alabama playing Auburn in front of seventy-five thousand cheering fans instead of just a bunch of kids in our backyard.

We wrote up stories about the games, too, and put them into the neighborhood newspaper we published and sold to everyone in the area. I guess if I did an accounting, I would find that I still owe the subscribers issues of the paper that they paid for but never received. Truth is, I quickly realized that newspaper publishing did not push the same buttons as sports, music, or other facets of show biz. I just did the paper for the money—and to drive attendance to our games, shows, and amusement parks.

The older I got, the more music seemed to dominate my interest. Music and radio. I remember riding in my dad's pickup truck, his radio on one of the local stations or pulling in one of the big signals out of Birmingham or Atlanta. It was mostly country music, but then I would hear rock and pop and R&B and I couldn't get enough of it. At night, on our big radio at home, I began to notice that when the sun went down, there was a whole new array of AM stations that rode in on the skip. There was an even wider variety of music, and it only whetted my appetite for more of it. I learned the lyrics and added the latest Top 40 hits to the shows we were putting on out in the carport.

There was something else that drew me to those stations besides just the music. The personalities fascinated me. Some call them disk jockeys, or deejays, but the good ones were far more than that. Those guys seemed to be having so much fun doing what they were doing, and they were as much a part of the show as the records they played. They didn't get in the way of the music they were spinning—they added to it. Guys like John Landecker and Larry Lujack. Stations with call letters and slogans like "the Big 89, WLS, Chicago" or "the Mighty 690, WVOK" from Birmingham, with the commercials for its Shower of Stars concerts with an all-star lineup of the very people who were recording all that great music. "Quixie in Dixie, WQXI, Atlanta." All AM stations. FM was not really there yet. Besides, I couldn't hear Chicago or Dallas or New York on FM. That dial was for elevator music anyway.

I loved to listen to those personalities every chance I got. There was a warmth to what those guys were doing, an excitement in their voices, a contagious zest that they applied to the music, to whatever they were talking about with their listeners, and even to the commercials they read. I caught myself flipping past the music sometimes, just to hear one of them do his act.

One of the area's best-known personalities, Gary Lee Love, from Q104 over in Gadsden—one of the first FM stations to have an impact—made an appearance one night at the local teen hangout, the Sunshine Skate Center in Oxford. He had long hair, a beard, and some cool half-glasses that just seemed to scream "Star!" He was a personality. People crowded around him. Some asked for an autograph. He played a few records for us to skate to, gave a couple of shout-outs, and was gone, but I was danged impressed with the whole thing.

You know what I believe it was that first attracted me so much to these radio personalities? It was one-on-one show business without having to go to all the trouble to assemble a band, rehearse, build sets, write a script, line off a field, sell tickets, put up curtains, or recruit reluctant kids to play bit parts. It was just the deejay, some records, and a microphone. A transmitter, too, if they wanted to be heard somewhere else besides the skating rink, but that wasn't really an impediment at first. Just doing it for the sake of doing it was enough.

At some point, though, it occurred to me that those guys broadcasting on the radio were getting paid to do what they were doing. I assumed they were being paid a lot to do it, too. Maybe millions of dollars!

The moment that concept hit me when I was about twelve years old, it was like a bright, bright light coming on.

Well, that part about the transmitter was quite the hurdle to overcome, but it didn't stop me. I tied an old tape cassette recorder microphone to a baseball bat, pulled my long-since-retired See-and-Say record player and the family console stereo together in a corner of the living room, stacked up what few records we had in the house, and put WXYZ on the air. I had deduced that the deejays—Malcolm Street and his son Rob Street on WHMA and local legend Rex Gardner, also on WHMA, some of the personalities I had heard on Dad's truck radio—had to be playing records on two turntables in order to mix them together the way they did. I suppose I had seen pictures of deejays somewhere to get some idea of how they had their studios set up, and I mimicked them the best I could with duct tape, the ball bat, and my mother's coffee table.

I alternated "shifts" with Greg, playing over and over the few "hits" we had, doing our own patter between the songs, ad-libbing commercials for the same businesses we heard on the local radio

My first shot at afternoon drive on WHMA AM 1390 in Anniston, Alabama. It appears the dress code was very flexible on the weekends.

stations or reading ads out of the newspapers. We recorded ourselves and played it all back so we could go to supper without signing the station off the air when the sun went down, like WVOK in Birmingham had to do.

Oh, we still had our neighborhood band going, putting on shows in the carport. Just putting up with our practicing should get our mom into the Mother Hall of Fame. Greg and I were both self-taught musicians. Dad wouldn't spring for a drum set, so I managed to save up fifty bucks for my first set and started banging away until I figured out how to play them.

The beagles were getting a rest by then, no longer called upon to perform in the circus. Sports had come along, too, and I played baseball, basketball, and football, which seriously cut down on the performances of the Burgess Family Flying Circus and the broadcast day of WXYZ.

There was no doubt about it. The hook had been set. I knew in my heart of hearts that I wanted to spend the rest of my days in some branch of show business, and radio seemed like a good possibility. I just had no idea how to get there—how to get onstage to sing and play, how to get a record cut and on the radio, how to get a job behind a microphone, spinning those records for an eager bunch of adoring listeners. I just knew I desperately wanted to go there, to perform before crowds, hear the roar of

Rick on 7th grade football team. This was really the first year that I started to realize I could play this game.

11

approval, to entertain thousands of listeners who would hang on my every clever word—to get paid millions of dollars for doing something I craved so fiercely that it bordered on an obsession.

I got a smidgen—Southern for a "little bit"—of it when I bluffed my way into a job as a deejay at the local teen club. I spun up a bald-faced lie and told the manager that I knew how to cue up and mix records and run the sound equipment. Somehow I figured it all out before he realized I was making up all my deejay expertise. It was there that I got just a touch of what it felt like to be "broadcasting," to be playing to an actual crowd of people who were not my neighbors at Cheaha Acres or family members who had no choice but to sit and watch and listen. But since I had sports and school to occupy most of my time, it was short-lived, and I still had no means of reaching that vague goal I had established for myself of being in the spotlight—onstage or on the radio—and famous.

Then I realized that the most obvious way to my dream was right there in front of me. Sports. Remember, "sports" equals "entertainment." So I threw myself into the one other thing that I seemed born to do, and a means to that end that appeared to be a reasonable possibility.

Okay, so I would be a football star. That would be my path to stardom, roaring crowds, millions of dollars.

Let the acclaim begin.

2 Radio in a Jug

The alarm clock is set to go off at 3:50 a.m. Monday through Friday at the Bussey house. If I—Bubba—am not at the studio by 5:00 a.m.—an hour before airtime—then I consider myself officially late. I like to get there in time to settle in and get ready for the show. The alarm clock is far enough from the bed that I have to pretty much get completely out of the sack to reach it and shut it off, or to hit the snooze for an extra ten minutes. If I don't get out of bed and shut it off, my lovely wife, Betty, is not above kicking me lovingly right out onto the floor so I will stop all the noise and allow her to sleep another few hours.

Even after all these years, I still worry that I will over-sleep some morning, though I have only been "late"—later than 5:00 a.m.—a couple of times. And I realize that Rick and Speedy and the rest could probably run the show just fine until I straggled in, but I can't help it. It's just something so ingrained in my soul that I could never deny it.

For a while I even used to have a diesel pickup truck with a timer that could be set to start the engine at a certain hour. I parked it near the bedroom window each night and had it set to crank itself up at 4:20 so it would wake me up. That was just in case the power went off or both Betty and I slept through the clock alarm.

It is my work ethic, true. But part of it is I still love doing this so much. I'm amazed that I am able to do what I do for a living. Getting up at 3:50 in the morning is a small sacrifice to make to be able to keep doing it.

But I don't mind it that I get paid to do it, too.

⸻

There is no doubt about it. I inherited my strong sense of duty—doing more than enough to earn my keep, taking responsibility, always doing the right thing, giving my all for whoever was paying me, always being early to wherever it was that I was supposed to be—from my parents. My father was a World War II veteran, serving with General Douglas MacArthur in the Philippines, but that was not something he talked about. Not even a little bit. Even though all his relatives and friends were outdoorsmen and hunters, he had no interest in that sort of thing. He told us, "I've spent enough time in the woods."

By "woods" he meant "jungle." That was about all he would say on the subject.

Instead he threw himself into work at a local factory in east Alabama, in Anniston, not far from where we lived in Jacksonville. He was doing the best he could to make a living for my mother and me. That seemed to be his only ambition. Even though he was a hardworking, no-nonsense kind of man, he wasn't mean or severe, just practical and down-to-earth. In his mind, power steering and air-conditioning in a vehicle were unnecessary frills.

I did learn that he was a cook in the service. The few times he tried to prepare meals for us at home, they were not so great, though. It turns out that was because there were only three of us instead of the hundreds at a time he cooked for in the military. He simply could not get the measurements right for our little family. He often prepared wonderful meals for church, though. So long as he was cooking for four hundred people and stirring scrambled eggs in a vat with a boat paddle, he was a master chef.

One day at his job, well before I came on the scene, Dad was involved in a terrible accident, one that could easily have taken his life. A long tray that carried molten metal broke loose and spilled the mass onto the floor near where he worked, splashing onto his legs and feet. He instinctively tried to scrape the hot metal off with his hands, badly burning them as well.

Combine those awful injuries, his arthritis, and the cancer that eventually took him from us when I was fourteen, and I don't think he spent another pain-free day in his life after the accident. Even so, I don't remember him ever complaining about his condition. I really wish I could have known him before his injuries and illnesses.

Later I learned that he did have a few pleasures in life. Those included listening to country music on the radio, playing a little music himself, and watching me participate in sports. He had a beat-up old guitar and would play and sing the songs of his idols: Johnny Cash, Hank Williams, and Gene Autry. Even after his hands were so badly burned at the plant, he still managed to eke out some chords on the guitar, though it had to be awkward and hurt him tremendously to do so. It eventually caused him to put the guitar away and never play it again.

Somewhere along the way he found out that a neighbor had a machine that allowed people to record sound right onto a vinyl disk. The device made an actual record that could then be played back on any turntable, just like a regular recording bought from Woolworth's. Using the neighbor's living room as a studio, he committed several songs to the disks and then promptly put them away. I don't know what he planned to do with those homemade recordings, but to my knowledge, he never let anybody else listen to them. They just got stored away in that closet, and Mom and I forgot about them.

Maybe the spark was lit by all my hours of listening to the radio with my dad, or maybe it was me as a young kid trying to figure out how that machine of his could plow grooves into vinyl and then reproduce real music we could sit and listen to as it was being played back. Whatever it was, a fire had been kindled inside me that would burn for the rest of my life. From an early age, gadgets, gizmos, space travel, and anything electronic fascinated me to no end.

Santa Claus brought me a set of Space Scout walkie-talkies for Christmas one year. That certainly fanned the flames. It was the technical side of things—how things worked—that caught my interest from as long as I can remember, and that cheap set of two-way radios was one of the earliest chances for me to experiment with electronics and radio.

Oh, I liked music just fine. Not necessarily the country music my dad loved so much, but rock and roll and the new disco dance music that was getting popular. Still, when I was with my dad, riding around in his car, the dial was usually on WANA, the AM country music station in nearby Anniston. That is, if the sun was up. He loved listening to Marvelous Marvin McCullough, a true local radio star. He was one of those deejays who made you feel that you actually knew him personally, even if you had never even seen him in person. It was as if he was playing those songs just for you, and telling you and you alone about the big sale at the A&P, so you could take advantage of the amazing bargains you could find there every week.

But once the sun had gone down, WANA faded away for us up in Jacksonville, and Dad turned the knob on the dashboard radio to 650, down at the left-hand side of the dial. There he could pull in the distant signal from WSM in Nashville, Music City USA. Or crank it up the other way and pull in WCKY from Cincinnati, Ohio. He would sometimes take the long way back home just so we could hear the last verse and chorus of a Porter Wagoner song or catch the last few minutes of Ralph Emery interviewing Webb Pierce about his latest song or tour.

Somewhere along the way, Dad brought home one of the oddest devices I have ever seen. I still don't know where or why he got it.

It was a radio in a jug. Like a ship in a bottle, this was an actual radio, encapsulated somehow in a huge glass jug. Had the jug contained something else besides a radio, it would have easily held ten gallons. If my dad wasn't listening to it, I was trying to figure out how that radio got in there. Or why anybody would even want to do such a thing.

Often at night, instead of turning on the flickering TV with its wavy picture barely making the trek from Birmingham or Atlanta, he would listen to WSM and other faraway stations. It was always country or gospel music that he sought out, though. Or sometimes he would still pull that guitar from its case and, despite the obvious pain, strum it and sing the same songs the deejays were playing through the static and fades of those far-flung radio stations.

He never said it out loud to my mother or me, but I now understand that somewhere in that practical, no-nonsense mind of his, there was a dream of someday singing on the radio, of being on the air in Nashville, like Porter or Webb.

Of course, it was never to be.

I would not have noticed that then. I was too busy being a typical kid, making up sports with the other kids in the neighborhood, spending time during the summers at my grandparents' farm, and learning to drive on their tractor. My papaw, Chester Gidley, put me up on that tractor when I was ten years old and let me drive it all over the place. He didn't share my mom's belief that anything a kid might do was likely to end up in disaster. He came from the "throw them in the water and they'll either learn to swim or drown" school of instruction. I hope the statute of limitations has run out on Papaw Gidley's driver's ed!

He is also the one who first got me to eat a fried chicken liver.

That culinary discovery led to a lifetime of pleasure. The chicken liver, when fried correctly, is about as good as it gets. It's still one of my favorite foods. Of course, there are those who say you could fry a rock and I would eat it, and they may be correct. If you give me ketchup with it, that is.

By the time Papaw taught me to drive, I had already recovered from being abandoned by my mother at a place called "school" when I started first grade. I took that separation hard, being an only child and having my mom all to myself. I quickly noticed, though, that there was a different kind of kid there, a softer kind of little person, and it was called a "girl." And as soon as I got over the shock, I quickly claimed one of them as my girlfriend. That is, after I got over my crush on one of my first-grade teachers. I then decided that this school thing was not so bad after all.

Caption to come

Even as a kid, I had a habit of taking things apart to see how they worked. I was especially curious about walkie-talkies. One day I was communicating to my buddy next door—via Space Scout walkie-talkies—some vital piece of top-secret military intelligence, when I heard my own voice coming weakly from my dad's radio-in-a-jug. I suppose I had left it turned on the night before and the skip station was no longer there at that spot on the dial, hogging the frequency during the daylight hours.

But how could that be? How could the walkie-talkie be coming through on the regular radio? What miraculous thing was this?

I told my buddy to stand by while I raced to my dad's big tool-box—the one I was supposed to never touch—and got a Phillips head screwdriver. With my tongue between my teeth in concentration, I carefully took the walkie-talkie case apart.

It looked just as it always had before when I probed around inside it. Yes, I had taken it apart many times, trying to figure out how it worked its simple magic. Then I noticed that a tiny screw—probably left loose inside from a previous visit—had become lodged in the windings of a small coil inside the plastic case. I removed it, put the thing back together, pushed the "talk" button, and called my friend.

He heard me just fine on his walkie-talkie, but I noticed immediately that I could no longer hear myself on the radio-in-a-jug. I carefully replaced the little silvery screw amid the coil wires, placing it exactly where it had been lodged before. Then I pushed the talk button again. There I was, plain as day, coming out of the radio speaker, just like Marvelous Marvin McCullough from down in Anniston, and Ralph Emery, all the way from WSM in Music City USA.

Tingling all over with excitement, I began experimenting, moving the screw around on the coil until the signal got louder. Then I told my friend to run over and turn a radio in his house to the same spot on the dial as the radio-in-a-jug was tuned. And to quit asking why and just go do it.

He could hear me on his house radio, too! All the way to next door, coming out of the same spot on the dial as a real radio station might be.

I was broadcasting!

I would like to say the clouds parted and there was a chorus of angels to signal this amazing revelation, but there was not, of course. It did mean, however, that WJAA (for Jacksonville State University, the University of Alabama, and Auburn University—because even then, I saw the value of trying to please as much of the audience as I could) was officially on the air.

Like Rick, I confiscated what record players I could from around the house. But being the deejay, like Marvelous Marvin McCullough, was not my real desire. I let my friend announce anytime he wanted to. In addition to worrying my mom to death about buying me fresh 9-volt batteries so we could keep the "station" on the air, I kept experimenting with the little radios, trying to cast a signal even farther out, maybe even to the end of the block!

Imagine that. People driving up my street or in their houses cooking supper would be able to tune in to WJAA!

It was about then in my busy childhood that I developed two other powerful interests in addition to walkie-talkie broadcasting and those soft people called "girls."

I saw Neal Armstrong take that one great leap for mankind right there on

Caption to come

the flickering black-and-white TV picture in our living room. Space and all the possibilities of our going there again and again fascinated me. Shortly after that momentous event, I secluded myself in the Bussey basement and manufactured a lunar module out of scraps of wood and a complete, new, unopened roll of my mother's aluminum foil. The module was huge and took up a good portion of our basement. Big enough that I could actually climb inside. I was still trying to figure out how to get it outside and launch it into orbit when my mother literally stumbled upon it down there.

Maybe it's denial, but I don't remember who was maddest: my mother, because she needed some of what she called "tinfoil" for something she was baking and didn't have any left, or my dad, simply because I had wasted something that he considered to be of value—even if it was only scrap pieces of lumber—doing something that wasn't really necessary.

No matter. I had made up my mind that I would become an astronaut and walk in Armstrong's footsteps in the lunar dust. I figured I would be on the moon before I finished high school and on Mars shortly after college.

That love of space travel, specifically, and science, in general, stayed with me. It even eventually guided me in my choice of what to study in college. And I still grab onto anything to do with NASA and the space program. The radio show has allowed me to get to know a number of the brilliant people who continue to send men and women into space, and I love to visit with them and soak up just a drop or two of their knowledge.

My other passion was baseball.

I really liked other sports, but it was baseball that drew me in. I had always—since the very beginnings of Little League—been an average player, usually ending up in right field. The truth is, I was afraid of the ball. Eventually I got better and found my way out of right field and into the infield.

I wanted to play football, too, but my parents were afraid I would get hurt. Maybe that's an only-child thing, being overly protective. My dad was also adamant, however, that if I started something, I would have to finish it. I suspect he thought I might not love playing football as much as I did baseball, and he didn't want me to have to persevere in something to which I was not totally committed. Quitting wouldn't have been an option once I started.

Because of his injuries, Dad could never really play catch with me, but I threw plenty with my friends and cousins. By the time I was twelve, I had outgrown my fear of the baseball somewhat and was getting to play more.

I dreamed of being a pitcher. However, one goal eluded me.

The curveball.

I decided that if I could throw the curve, they would have to let me pitch. No matter how hard I tried, though, I could not get the ball to break. The coaches told me to just give up, to stop trying before I ruined my arm. But I kept trying anyway. Then I put liniment on my aching shoulder and tried some more. Still, no matter how hard I envisioned batters whiffing pitifully at my long, sweeping, breaking curveball, I couldn't conjure up the right physics to make that baseball do what I so desperately wanted it to do.

Then a miraculous thing happened. I broke my arm in phys ed

class at school. No, that wasn't the miracle. In fact, I figured that would put an end once and for all to my pitching fantasy, and I was really depressed about it. It helped that the girls seemed to feel sorry for me and crowded around to sign my cast, but that didn't make up for the fact that my career with the Atlanta Braves was so rudely sidetracked.

No, the amazing thing was—just like that kid in the movie who suddenly developed major-league pitching ability after an injury—that when the cast came off my pitching arm, I could suddenly throw the most beautiful curveball you have ever seen. Beautiful, that is, if you are not the batter!

Soon it was my go-to pitch. At the age of twelve, I was a pretty

Caption to come

good pitcher and, in my mind, mere steps now away once more from the starting rotation for the Atlanta Braves.

I had a new immediate goal. Armed with the curveball, I now aspired to pitch a no-hitter. That was the ultimate in baseball. A perfect game, considering the likelihood of an error or other flub among a bunch of kids, was virtually impossible. But I knew I could pitch a no-hitter, and I vowed I would not stop until I did.

My dad would tell me, "Bill, just win the game."

Still, I swear that I saw a twinkle in his eye when he said it, as if he would take special pride if I could somehow manage to pull off a perfect game. I can't remember him or my mom ever missing one of my games, unless he was in the hospital. For a man who put little stock in anything unnecessary or in wasting time on anything that wasn't considered "work," he really enjoyed watching me play. He would bring a lawn chair from home to sit in because it hurt his feet so badly to climb up onto those bleachers.

He would settle down there behind the backstop, not yelling or cheering. Instead, he watched every pitch. Then afterward, on the way home or over supper, he seemed to forget the pain for a while and whatever it was that happened in the war that he did not want to talk about. We would dissect the game, and he never failed to give me encouragement.

I was in the thirteen-to-fifteen-year-old league, having a great season and flirting often with that elusive no-hitter. That was when my dad suddenly got sick.

Almost overnight he developed ugly knots on his neck and back and was in even more pain than usual. The doctors diagnosed him with non-Hodgkin's lymphoma, an especially aggressive cancer. He endured some rugged rounds of chemotherapy that left him sick and drained. Ironically, though, that poison seemed to make his arthritis better. Once he got over the sickness from the chemo, he actually felt better than he had in years. That, of course, didn't last long.

I tried to talk him into letting me quit the team. I felt that I should be there with Mom, helping her when he was in the hospital or too weak from the chemo and cancer to take care of himself.

"No!" he told me. He made it very clear. "You start something, you finish it. You are a part of a team, and you will not let them down."

I am sure that one way I dealt with my dad's declining health was to throw myself totally into baseball. He still came to see me play when he felt up to it. I would be out there on the mound, warming up, and could hear him coming. He was simply too weak to lift the lawn chair. It made an awful racket as he dragged it behind him in the loose gravel of the parking lot. I can't imagine the pain he was feeling, how sick he must have been, but he still showed up at the ball field, dragging that lawn chair. Then, as usual, he sat there quietly, studying every pitch, glaring at the umpire if he thought he missed a call.

We knew the end was near. He was in the hospital, probably never to come home again, when I finally threw that no-hitter. That night the curve was amazing. The fastball was smoking. I had done it! I pitched the game of my life. Even though my father had been unconscious for several days, mostly hallucinating or in a near coma, unaware even of who was in the room, I couldn't wait to get there and try to tell him about the game.

I rushed to the hospital, holding the scuffed, grass-stained game ball firmly wrapped up in my glove. I could only hope he would be awake and lucid so I could let him know I had finally done it.

My dad was unconscious and died later that night.

I had become a Christian five years earlier, when I was ten years old, at a revival service in Weaver, Alabama. Even then, at that young age, I understood Jesus and His message to us all about personal responsibility and that Christ is the only way to the Father. Without hesitation, I walked down the aisle to the altar at that little country church to accept Jesus as my Savior.

Understand that when I needed emotional comfort, like most kids, I had always turned to my mother. Dad was so matter-of-fact, so duty-bound; I knew I would get little sympathy from him. But at the revival service that Sunday, when I decided I was saved and ready to be baptized and wanted to publicly accept Jesus as my personal Savior, I walked right over to the pew where my parents sat and told Dad I wanted him to walk up there with me.

And he did. He held my hand all the way up the aisle and knelt next to me at the altar. I remember it as if it happened yesterday, and I am still thankful that I could share that moment with my dad.

During those rides in his Ford Maverick, we had sometimes talked about God, about Dad's own religious beliefs and his personal relationship with God. They were not something he wore on his sleeve. He had a deep understanding of theology, but he also knew how to make it simple enough for even a young man to understand. His principles were basic but firm. God was the Father. Jesus was the Son. God sent his Son to die for our sins. The least we could do is live our lives in a way that would show we appreciated that amazing sacrifice.

Father to son, the way he explained it to me, it made perfect sense. You know what? It still does.

The day we buried my dad, and just before they closed the lid on his coffin, I walked up and put my scuffed-up, grass-stained, no-hitter baseball into his scarred hand. It never bothered me that he didn't hear about my no-hitter before he died.

See, he knows. He certainly knows.

Many years later, Mom and I found some of those old vinyl records he made of himself singing and playing the guitar. I transferred them to a compact disc for safekeeping.

I had the CD with me at the radio studio one morning. It was the Friday before Father's Day. On a whim, we were goofing around and decided to play some of them on the air during the show. It was an emotional moment for me, but then I had a thought that almost did me in, right there on the radio and in front of hundreds of thousands of people out there in the listening audience.

I suddenly realized we had a station that carried our show in Nashville. In an odd way, my dad's dream had finally come true.

He was able to sing on the radio in Music City USA.

3 Too Good for Division II

I am pretty sure that one of the main reasons Bubba and I have been successful with the show is that we simply out-work everybody else. We show up every day, we're on time, we do the finest show we can possibly do, and when the show is over, if we don't feel like we've been carrying bricks or chopping wood all day, we haven't done our best. There are people who depend on us to work as hard as we can, much as teammates on a sports team do.

There is talent involved, I guess. A lot of luck, too. But we both recognize that if we don't do our best, if we don't work hard, somebody else with more talent may just come in and outwork us and leave us battered and bloody and defeated when the final score is posted.

Then I will have to go back to being the fill-in deejay at the skating rink to feed my family.

———

I was lucky. I inherited good football genes. That allowed me to be a pretty good football player, even with minimal effort on my part. Truth is, I coasted all the way through high school, relying entirely on those lucky genes. Why bother with effort if I could be an all-star on one of the best high school teams in the state and get attention from a bunch of Southeastern Conference football powers that wanted to

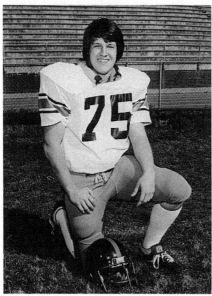

Senior year, Oxford High School football, ol' 75

hand me a free college education? A scholarship that would allow me to play—be in the spotlight—in front of thousands of people in the stands and millions watching on television every Saturday afternoon in the fall.

Of course, I was blessed with one of the best coaches in the state, too. I remember one of those unbelievably hot August days, in the middle of two-a-day practices. That was when we were out there on the field from daylight to midmorning and then came back from three in the afternoon until it was too dark to see the other end of the field when we ran our gassers. We had been running wind sprints beneath the blazing sun one day until we were praying for the Lord to send us a heatstroke, just so we could maybe get some relief during the ambulance ride to the hospital. Dad had decided—correctly in my case—that we were loafing, and he was going to run us until we gave the required effort or dropped.

"Jacksonville ain't loafing! Anniston ain't loafing! They're running through their wind sprints right about now, all the way through the end zone, and then they are lining up again, begging for more," he preached. I knew he was talking to the entire team, but I couldn't help but think he was really aiming his sermon directly at me. "That's how they'll beat your tails in the playoffs, if we even get that far. They won't quit at the 10-yard line and coast the rest of the way! You can mark that up! They won't quit because they want to win the game more than you do."

That was when several of us noticed that he was standing in the middle of a bed of fire ants, the most vicious insect God ever created. His legs were covered in the things, and they had to be biting him already.

"Coach, you're in an ant bed," we told him.

He did not even flinch. Never moved. Did not acknowledge those biting varmints even existed.

"I don't have time to worry about that, and neither do you. You can't worry about the heat or getting hurt. That's what I'm talking about! We got some more gassers to run if we want to be around, still in the game in the fourth quarter at Gadsden."

The only thing I knew was that my God-given genes promised to

31

allow me to be involved in something that provided me a stage before cheering crowds, beneath bright lights, and with lots and lots of attention. Oh, I was still interested in radio and music, but for the time being, football gave me those things I most craved.

Never mind that I was an all-C student. Tennessee, Mississippi State, Vanderbilt (who had apparently not yet inspected my transcript), and Auburn—all from the mighty Southeastern Conference—were keeping our mailbox at home full. It was good to be wanted by so many, and you can believe that I ate it up.

Senior year football, fall 1982. Pictured with Mickey Shadrix. We would soon be doing my first ever morning show: Rick and Mick.

We had a great year and we ultimately faced a big Birmingham-area school—Gardendale—in the second round of the playoffs. They were undefeated and ranked number one in the state. I was going up against Kurt Jarvis, a tremendous player who eventually started for Alabama and played in the NFL. It was the perfect opportunity for old

Rick to forget about the rest of the team and show all the colleges and sportswriters just how good he was.

Believe it when I tell you that I was having a great game, too. That is, until I got tangled up in a double-team block and it felt as if my leg had been caught in a hay baler. I limped to the sidelines, got taped up, and went right back in, but it wasn't the same after that.

In the stands that night was Pat Dye, the head coach of the Auburn Tigers. He had been one of my most persistent suitors. I was certain that after the game I had that night, despite the ligament damage I suffered and because of the toughness I showed by limping back into the game, I would have in hand the offer of a full-ride scholarship to play for the Tigers.

It was not to be.

The other schools had already backed off. Rumor was that since I had a strong Auburn connection because of my dad (who went to school and played there), I had already decided to go to college and play there. The other schools took their scholarship offers off the table. Whether it was the injury in the Gardendale game or that Coach Dye believed he had me locked up already, he made an offer I never expected: no scholarship, no " full ride," but I was welcome to walk on, play a year, and possibly receive a scholarship later.

Now Play-the-Field Rick was Slapped-in-the-Face Rick. I admit it. My pride was hurt.

I had an alternative, though. Troy State University, then a small NCAA Division II school, stepped in and made me a full-ride offer. To their credit, my dad and mom let me make the decision. There was something to be said for somebody liking me enough that they would give me a full scholarship when somebody else—the team I really wanted to play for—did not. I took Troy State's offer.

I guess I didn't realize how far from Auburn or Alabama or Tennessee Troy State was back then. I received an invitation to play in the state high school all-star game in Tuscaloosa that next summer before starting to college. When the players who had signed with the big schools were introduced to the crowd, huge numbers of those in attendance stood and whooped like crazy for the ones headed for careers at their favorite schools. But when they introduced old number 75, Rick Burgess, headed to Troy State, only my mother stood and cheered.

Something else profound happened while I was in Tuscaloosa for that all-star game. I had my first real encounter with Big Red—our name for Satan.

There was plenty of partying going on there, with so many of us away from home for the first time. At one point someone handed me a cold beer. Believe it or not, I had never tasted the stuff before. I don't want to make more of it than I should, but that first beer knocked me right off the path, and it took me thirteen years to get back on track.

To this point I had been a "cultural Christian," going to church, never missing Sunday school. I had been baptized already, too, and since I'd never had a beer or smoked a cigarette, I felt like I was doing all God required of me. Between church, school, football, and my odd jobs, I simply had never had the time to try the sins I am sure most other high school kids got tempted with.

Troy State had made a big sacrifice, giving a scholarship to me that could have gone to someone else, but I don't think I was aware of that fact. All I knew was that I was playing before smaller crowds than I had in high school, and that wasn't motivating for me. Even though I was getting lots of playing time in my freshman year, the whole experience was unfulfilling. I was depressed and did not give it much effort. I still relied on my genetics to get me through, not any special effort. I should have been playing before ninety thousand people over at Auburn. They should have been talking about my wonderful defensive plays on national television. I had convinced myself that old number 75 was simply too good for little Troy State University and NCAA Division II.

In pursuit of my first college quarterback sack. Troy State, fall 1983, against Valdosta State. My football days were numbered. I left the team the following summer of 1984.

I discovered something else that I was good at. If there was a party, I found it. Man, I could tell jokes, sing, act a fool, and be the center

35

of attention at every fraternity throw-down or keg party there was. I made up for all the sinning I missed back in high school.

Class? What class? You mean they expected me to play ball, be the life of every party within fifty miles, *and* go to class?

Needless to say, I left Troy and moved back home after one year. I enrolled at Jacksonville State University, just up the road, and, with football behind me, immediately started looking for alternative forms of limelight to shine brightly on my show-business craving.

I found it at WLJS, 92J, the campus radio station at Jax State. It was a real live FM radio station that could actually be heard for a few miles beyond the school, not a playlike station in our carport or a booth at the teen club. When I told them about my vast experience behind the turntables, they gave me a shift. On the air. In the mornings, when people might actually tune in and listen to me. I was so thrilled with the prospects that I forgot the part about getting paid.

I had hooked back up with a friend from high school, Mickey Shadrix, who shared my passion for radio, and we decided to do a two-man show, spinning the hits and doing our disk jockey act.

Nothing had ever felt so right. No, I mean it. I had found my calling, even if it didn't pay a dime and was on a low-power college radio station in the middle of rural Alabama.

It didn't have the frustrations of being in a band—rehearsing, trying to find someone to let us play, or having to write our own songs because we were not good enough to play the ones written by other people. Mickey was a good partner, too, without all the ego clashes and infighting that inevitably happen in a band.

With our show we could crack the microphone open and talk, say clever things, be spontaneous, and actually have people hear what we were putting out there. Listeners called in and requested songs and told us they were enjoying the program at this or that sorority house or dorm or apartment complex.

I took my inspiration from other two-man shows I was hearing as FM was finally making serious inroads against the old AM power-houses. People like Rick Zisk and Dennis Deason on the mighty Q104, easily the most popular station in our area by that time. Or Mark and Brian on I-95 in Birmingham, to this day major personalities in Los Angeles. ("Come money, come. Come money, come." More on that little chant later.) The Rick and Mick Show on 92J sounded similar to those, and there was a good reason. If those guys were successful at this radio thing, then we would steal their act, put our own spin on it, and make it ours.

We must have done something right—or maybe we were the only idiots willing to get up early for no salary and do a radio show—but management kept us in the morning slot. That was the first time I had any idea that this was the "money" shift. I had always listened to the guys at night, playing to a young audience, but then I realized that Rick and Dennis, Mark and Brian, and Rick Dees (another Birmingham personality who went on to do very well in Los Angeles and in national syndication) were all morning shows.

And so was Mickey's and my little program.

Though a campus station, we had commercials, jingles, and what we in radio call a "format," guidelines on what you can play and say, often dictated by upper management based on expensive advice from a "broadcast consultant." That was my first experience with someone telling me how to behave on the air, what music to play, and in what order. It was a lot different from WXYZ, "broadcasting" from my bedroom.

I immediately decided this format thing—other people trying to tell me what to do—put a serious crimp in what I did. I knew better and began exploring ways to stretch the limits. After all, I was already doing that very thing in other areas of my life, so why not in my budding broadcast career?

There was another rub. Mickey was a wonderful human being, strong in faith. He conducted himself in the way of people who exhibit their love of the Lord by the way they live, not by telling others how to conduct their lives. I, on the other hand, continued to drink and party and live the lifestyle I figured all major radio personalities did. It was already having an effect on me, if not on the show.

Young and strong or not, it is hard to party all night and show up at six in the morning and still be on top of your game. That led to some uncomfortable moments, but I was having so much fun, I hardly noticed.

Though he has probably questioned his sanity many times since, it was my dad who helped me get me my first real, paying job in radio. Of course, as a popular high school football coach, he was quite well-known in the area. He was friends with the manager of one of the stations in nearby Anniston, WHMA-AM. I heard through the grapevine that they were looking for someone to work weekends, run taped programs, man the board when Paul Harvey or the Atlanta Braves play-by-play was on the air, and do odd jobs around the station. Dad agreed to mention me to his friend.

When they offered me the job, I was thrilled beyond belief. I was going to be on a commercial radio station! "Be on" meaning I had been told not to even turn on the microphone switch, to just play the tapes and commercials, the network feeds and Atlanta Braves baseball games, and otherwise shut up. But regardless, I would be giving up my amateur status. Someone was going to pay me money to work in radio!

Not much money. Even though he had played a role in my first big career move, my dad was less than impressed when I told him the tiny hourly wage I would soon be making as a radio star.

"Rick, I would not even cross the street for that kind of money," he snapped. "Why don't you pay attention in school, stay at the campus station until you get it all out of your system, and then get a real job when you graduate?"

Coming from him, it was like a slap in the face to me. I always wanted his approval, and he had just denied it for something that meant a great deal to me.

Later that same day, he called me aside.

"Son, I want to apologize," he told me, looking me squarely in the eye. "I was wrong in what I said this morning." You would have to know my dad to understand how big a confession this was. And what a profound impact it had on me. "You made a big step to do something you love to do, and you got the job on your own merits. It is something you are passionate about, and I should support you in that. I just want you to know that I do."

He has supported me in every move I have made since then, though it couldn't have been easy at times. Advised, argued, bit his tongue, but always supported my decision. That is love, and I am convinced that short, sweet talk that day ultimately made me a better father and a better man.

Meanwhile I continued to work at 92J with Mickey, ran tapes at the Anniston station, and sometimes "accidentally" had to open the microphone and say something on the air. I hoped for bad weather or breaking news so I could do my thing.

I also partied hardily, never missing a beat there. I even managed to show up for class enough to squeak by on the way to my degree in, of all things, sociology, with a minor in radio and TV.

There was another snag when it came to school. In the sociology curriculum, I was required to take a foreign language.

Okay, I figured, let's do Spanish. How hard could it be? I had watched the Clint Eastwood westerns. I knew most of the Cheech and Chong comedy bits by heart. Zorro was one of my favorites.

The teacher in the class I took was Mrs. Suco, a brave lady whose family fled Cuba ahead of dictator Fidel Castro to start a new life in America. I'm convinced that trying to teach me how to speak Spanish made her strongly consider returning to Havana and taking her chances with Fidel and Godless communism.

Yes, I admit that I didn't take the class very seriously. Something about saying things in another tongue when I could much more easily say them in good old English made it all seem a waste of time. I figured I could manage to find food with a mention of "taco" or "burrito." Besides, why did a radio star need to know how to speak Spanish?

I claim to have learned only one Spanish phrase, and I applied it to any situation that arose.

¿Donde está el baño? Where is the bathroom?

Hey, that could be a valuable bit of language to have available, pro-viding whoever you are asking just points and doesn't give directions verbally.

There was another fellow in that class with me, a guy who was struggling just as mightily with Romance languages as I was. I knew who he was already but had never really met him before that first day of class. We knew some of the same people and almost certainly hung out in some of the same places while growing up. I played football with a couple of his cousins at Oxford, but he had gone to Jacksonville High, a hated rival that we beat soundly on a consistent basis.

He didn't seem to hold that athletic domination against me and seemed to be an okay guy. In fact, we hit it off right away. Just hearing him say, "*¿Donde está el baño?*" in the most profound Southern accent you have ever heard absolutely owned me. I soon found that he also had an interest in doing something in radio broadcasting, but that he was more interested in the technical side than in being on the air. I didn't understand that at all, but I liked him nonetheless.

Truth is, we kept each other from going loco in Spanish class even as we drove poor Mrs. Suco crazy. We had instant chemistry and kept each other—as well as most of the other students in the class—laugh-ing out loud with our antics, despite Mrs. Suco's best efforts to make us behave. (It's true that to this day Mrs. Suco refuses to acknowledge we were ever in any of her classes and will not do any interviews about those days. She has, to her credit, managed to sponge it right out of her memory.)

Finally, at the end of her rope, she decided one day to reseat the class, but this time to line up everyone alphabetically. It was, she figured, a good way to separate my new friend and me and to regain some control of her classroom. She obviously did not think through this move very well.

That is how I, Rick Burgess, came to occupy the desk right in front of Mr. Bill Bussey, the "Silver-Tongued One."

And the goofy stuff we came up with to avoid having to conjugate Spanish verbs in Mrs. Suco's class at Jacksonville State University were the first seeds of what would one day become the *Rick and Bubba Show*.

Muy bien!

4 Grit and Wisdom

I know I am the most unlikely radio personality there is likely to ever be. I don't have the voice for it. I have no training for it.

I just know that one day somebody is going to come into the studio, take a pair of wire cutters to my microphone cable, and say to me, "Bill 'Bubba' Bussey, exactly who do you think you're kidding with this radio announcer thing?"

Or that somebody who is willing to work just a little bit harder than I am will come storming in, push me aside, grab my spot, and take over.

There are plenty of people out there who have more talent than I do, but I plan on making certain nobody will ever work as hard at it as I do. Work comes naturally to me. So do grit and determination. Those things I inherited from my mom and dad.

And even if I don't have a deep voice or perfect diction, I'll use what I do have to win.

My mother grew up plowing fields on her family's dirt farm, not on a tractor but behind a mule. Her older brother, Clois Gidley, went to war, so she had no choice. There was nobody else to help her family bring in the crops, and if they were to eat and have clothes to wear, the work had to be done. She just did what she had to do when she plowed with that mule. When she got to the end of a row, she turned the animal around and headed for the other end of the field until the entire plot was plowed and planted. When she was seventeen, she lied about her age and got a job in a local factory. So there she was, when most kids her age were worrying about the prom or who was dating whom, carrying a lunch bucket to a full-time job. It didn't faze her, though.

That's why I always say I inherited my work ethic and my even-keel personality from my mom and my grittiness from my dad. I needed both after my dad died.

I love President Ronald Reagan, but he did some tricks with Social Security and how it affected dependents of deceased parents that left me out in the cold. In order to keep some benefits from my father coming in, I had to take college courses while I was still in high school. Turns out I enjoyed it, but it took a lot of time away from other things, like playing with my newfound interest in CB radio. And girls. I enrolled in college classes at Jacksonville State University and in radio and TV repair and electronics courses at Gadsden State Junior College at night.

All along I counted on getting a baseball scholarship to pay my way to college when I graduated high school. I am sure my mother would have liked it too.

My senior year we had a great baseball team. Colleges were already looking at a half dozen of us for scholarships. We even beat Oxford High, our main rival and Rick's school, two times that year. One time they had to invoke the mercy rule, and that had never happened before. We cruised to the league championship.

Then things fell apart. We had a player who hadn't been able to get advanced placement courses at his tiny little rural school, so he transferred to Jacksonville High for his senior year. He was, it turned out, also a pretty good baseball player. The state high school athletic association decided that his transfer to Jacksonville High was somehow illegal. They put us on probation, taking away a bunch of our wins.

That was disastrous. It meant we could not go to the state championship, losing exposure to college coaches and professional scouts. Six players on our team did get scholarships anyway. A couple who were "on the bubble," including Bill Bussey, did not get immediate offers.

I could have gone to a junior college and played baseball, but that would have meant leaving Mom at home by herself. She was after me to buckle down, to concentrate on school, a privilege she'd never had. So I tied up a baseball in my glove with a shoestring, just to keep it shaped, and sometimes rubbed it down with Neatsfoot oil to make sure it was supple, but my serious baseball-playing days were over.

Let me tell you, it took some grit to walk away from sports, and especially baseball, a game that had been so important to me all my life. Part of it was how much it meant to my dad in his last days. It took a lot of determination, as well, to give up on being an astronaut or pitching for the Braves, or both. I figured that was just a big part of growing up, though.

There was nothing directly related to electronics at Jax State, where I decided to go to school, so I gravitated to the next most technical thing: computers. I majored in computer science and eventually graduated with a degree in technology. You could spot us computer geeks right away, walking around with our stacks of punch cards. Diskettes and, certainly, flash drives were not around yet. I enjoyed learning about computers, but something else still pulled at me. Radio, especially the technical and business side of it.

I had discovered Citizens' Band radio as a kid, just about the time Burt Reynolds and Jerry Reed were making it so popular with *Smokey and the Bandit*. My uncle, Paul Bussey—who used the handle "the Chevron Man"—was big into it too. I was immediately attracted to the magical part of it, the casting signals around and bouncing them off the ionosphere—like my Space Scout walkie-talkies breaking through on our big radio. But there was also something enticing about the way the people on the airwaves told their stories and seemed to have such a special bond of friendship, all without actually seeing each other. Early on, Dad was totally opposed to my getting a CB radio, mostly because it would involve putting up what some might consider an ugly antenna outside of the house. I considered it to be true home improvement and a beautiful addition.

Between my uncle and me, we finally wore him down. I was about thirteen or fourteen when my mom and dad bought me a CB radio, and I came up with a mast and an antenna. I put it up in the backyard, the mast bracketed to the house. I kept the radio on my nightstand and went to bed at night listening to all the chatter, the people telling tall tales, and sometimes even distant voices with strange accents—I'm sure mine sounded strange to them, too!

I eventually got to meet in person many of the people I heard and talked with on the CB at their "coffee breaks." That is where groups get together for what they called "eyeball conversations." Let me tell you, that was the first time I realized people do not ever look the way they sound on the radio!

Like many others before me, I quickly moved to the hobby of amateur—or "ham"—radio. It required much more technical ability, and the signals could reach out much farther. Bill Cain, a neighbor with the call sign K4DXH, was a "ham," and he loaned me a copy of *Electronics Made Simple*. I gobbled it up. In the middle of school, girls, part-time jobs, girls, the skating rink, church, and girls, I also found time to take an electronics class. I eventually took the test and got my Federal Communications Commission amateur radio license. It is a pastime I still enjoy very much today, and I have many "ham" friends out there.

My experience with Citizens' Band and amateur radio was the launchpad for what I was sure was going to be a lifetime career as a radio engineer or some other kind of involvement in the technical and management side of communications. I knew I wanted to be in radio. I still had no thoughts at all of being *on* the radio.

By the time I got to college, the technical stuff was starting to make a lot of sense to me. Some of the other courses . . . well . . . not so much.

Spanish was one of them. I still don't know why a communications engineer needs to *habla español,* but there I was, in Mrs. Suco's class, lost in a maze of tildes and *vocabulario* and conjugations. The only thing that made it bearable was this big, funny guy named Rick. Rick Burgess. I sort of knew him already. One of my cousins played football with him at Oxford, and of course I knew he had been a ferocious football star who ate offensive linemen for lunch. I was aware of him being on the radio as a deejay on the campus FM station, too, but didn't know at first how serious he was about a career in radio.

Funny thing was, we saw things in the same fractured but hilarious way and kept each other laughing, much to the dismay of our serious, dedicated Spanish teacher. I soon learned how deep his interest was in broadcasting.

Mostly, though, I was just happy that I had somebody who shared my sense of humor and would help me get through what I was certain was going to be a boring class.

We somehow made it out of that semester without getting kicked out of college but also without knowing any more than a good dozen Spanish words between us. If either of us ever becomes stranded in Mexico, we could maybe get directions to a bathroom, but we would have a hard time doing anything else.

Although I still saw Rick around campus and heard him on 92J, the campus station, and eventually on the Anniston radio stations, I lost track of him for a while. But I never forgot him. I figured if he could help me endure Spanish class, if he could find humor in some of the situations we were in, then he had a future in show business.

The time was coming when I would develop one big honkin'

dream. I wanted to own a radio station. Not a Christmas walkie-talkie with a loose screw. An honest-to-goodness, over-the-air, moneymaking radio station.

And when I got that station, I knew who I wanted to be one of my disk jockeys. I was listening to him on the Anniston station, playing the hits and doing stuff just as funny as what he and I had come up with in Mrs. Suco's Spanish class.

Now all I had to do was find a way to obtain that radio station and begin building Bill Bussey's broadcasting empire of the air.

5   "Hello, You're on the Air!"

Unlike most people who have made their living in radio, I—Rick—have never once been fired from a job. Looking back, each move to another station was a positive one, jumping by choice to a better position, though I wondered about some of them at the time. There was always a reason.

Even Bubba and I have moved up and down the dial a time or two since we got together, but thankfully, most of the listeners always made the move with us.

God has a plan. Sometimes I wish He would take a minute to explain it to us and not make us rely totally on faith. Nevertheless, I figure that, too, is simply part of the plan. We just have to have patience and then, when we look back, we see things happened for a grander purpose.

If I was a tool of the Lord's in the late '80s, however, I have to wonder why He didn't take me back to Sears while I was still under warranty and get Himself a free replacement!

***

I was living the dream! Doing a radio show on 92J, working weekends and fill-in on WHMA-AM, playing in a band whenever I got the chance, going to school sometimes, laughing, drinking, partying. I had come a long way from deejaying at the teen club, and now, well, old Rick Burgess was the king of the broadcast world, all while working on being a rock-and-roll star. I even used 92J to promote a New Year's Eve dance I put together and to hype our band. We had named ourselves Mystique. We thought the name sounded cool and edgy at the time, but now I'm sure it probably reminded people more of a cheap perfume.

Still, invoking the power of radio, I used commercials to make it appear this would be a colossal event, much bigger than it really was, and it only cost three dollars per person. That was one of the great things about the medium. With some music and a big voice and production effects, you could make anything sound much grander than it actually was.

It worked. The place was packed. We rigged up our own pyrotechnics, using black powder and some bare electrical wires to ignite flash pots at the exact right moments during the show. It's a wonder that we didn't burn down the building, and I am sure we damaged some people's hearing that night. That was the first time, however, that the true power of radio hit home with me. If we could take our little band

and, with some well-done commercials, make it just as big an event as we made it sound, then there was a magic to this medium I had not really considered. If you act like something is a big deal, it just might turn out to be!

I learned something else during those band days that helped to form what the *Rick and Bubba Show* later became. One of our band members was a childhood friend named Chuck Mason. Not long after we renamed our group Silent Reign—after a bottle of my mother's White Rain shampoo—and while we were in New Orleans, about to record our first album, Chuck suddenly took sick. Through it all, however, he maintained the most wonderful sense of humor you could imagine, always keeping us laughing. And I noticed it was the real stuff that was the funniest, the most interesting.

When Chuck passed away, I lost interest in the band. My brother, Greg, was in the band, too, and we were both close to Chuck. Greg left to take a full-time job with the power company, climbing utility poles. I went back to radio. Silent Reign dried up.

Slowly but surely, I moved up at WHMA, from just weekends to doing a music show in the afternoons. I quickly dubbed it the *Afternoon Extravaganza*—make it a bigger deal than it really is, and it just might turn out to be one!—used my fake radio deejay voice, and figured I was on my way to stardom. I had started working some shifts on the sister station, WHMA-FM, too, mostly late nights and weekends, but my out-of-control lifestyle was starting to affect my job. I was still in school, too.

I came dashing in for my shift almost an hour late one night. I apologized to the young lady who had worked the seven-to-midnight slot. I knew she could smell the alcohol on me, so I didn't even try to lie or make excuses.

"Look, I'm sorry," I told her. "Cover for me with the program director, okay? I'll return the favor someday."

She had been talking with someone on the phone when I burst in. She started the next record, picked up the phone, and said to the person on the other end, loud enough for me to hear, "He's here. You want me to stop and get something to eat on my way home? All right. I will. Bye. Love you, too."

When she hung up, she turned to me.

"You all right to go on the air? I have to get my husband a sandwich. My husband, the program director."

I was lucky to keep my job after that one.

Then a door opened. The legendary Rex Gardner passed away, leaving his program vacant. It was a morning talk show called *On the Air*. Several others took the show for a while, including George Salmon, who would play a later role in my career. Then one day I learned the position was open again. I am still not sure what made me, a record-spinning disk jockey, do it—the hand of the Lord?—but I went to station management and volunteered to take over Gardner's old slot. No records, talk all the time, live commercials, selling advertising for the show. For some reason the management let me do it. And I found I loved it. Loved the freedom to say what I wanted to say, to interact with listeners on the telephone, to not be constrained by a format, a particular kind of music.

Even as I was messing up my personal life, I must have been doing something right on the radio. I got the call one day from a familiar voice, George Salmon, with whom I had worked at WHMA. He had come to Oxford to work for a new FM station that was preparing to go on the air, called K-98. It was an adult contemporary station and, with FM really starting to catch on, was sure to quickly build a sizable audience, even as WHMA-AM's was dwindling. He told me he had mentioned me to the station's owner, and they wanted to know if I would be interested in coming over to do the afternoon show on the new station.

I was flattered, but I had to think about it. The money was a whopping forty-five dollars a week more than I was making at WHMA-AM, and they were going to allow me to sell commercials, too. Not just for my show but for the whole station. And they were going to pay me 15 percent commission. I could make as much money as I wanted to.

There was a negative side. I would be back into formatted radio, playing what they wanted me to play. Locked into a type of music that set the tone for what I could do on the air.

I finally told K-98 that I would take the job. I still hadn't let go of the idea that the afternoon drive-time shift was the best there was, but it began to dawn on me—pun intended—that mornings might actually be where I should be, even if it required me to get out of bed early. I had finally realized that mornings offered more freedom to create and entertain. So when K-98 later offered me the morning show, I accepted it, with one condition. I could do the show the way I wanted. They agreed to my stipulation.

At that time, in the early '90s, country music ruled the airwaves in our area. Even the kids, the ones who had once loved rock and roll, were drifting off amid the "urban cowboy" influence on country music and radio. One of the first things I did at K-98 was to openly declare war on the big country stations. I came up with the "Friends don't let friends listen to country music" campaign. I renamed the country music superstar Garth Brooks "Garth Vader" and challenged him to come on the show and defend that twangy stuff he was throwing out there.

Well, I had touched a nerve. Apparently a lot of other people were not necessarily country music fans and they rallied around my cause. The show was developing a following. When I called on sponsors, they knew who I was and either agreed with my anti–country music stance or gave me a tough time about it. Either way, they bought ads because there were listeners to hear their messages.

I was still in my midtwenties, just graduated from college, so I didn't let the listeners know how young I was. I thought I was maturing pretty quickly anyway.

I should also mention here that along the way I had gotten married to a fellow broadcaster. We were both more about pursuing our radio careers than about our marriage, even though God had blessed us with two precious children. The truth is, I was living a lifestyle so dark that my mother even took me aside and told me that she questioned my salvation. My wife and I had no concept of holy matrimony. We divorced.

I had realized long before that the best radio stars did shows that were a direct reflection of their own personalities. One morning I was driving much too fast to try to get to work. The overnight deejay had already started the first record of my shift and I needed to get there before it ran out or it would be obvious to everyone that I was late.

That was when it struck me that my show in no way mirrored my life at the time. I was trying to be a shock jock, a young Howard Stern (the very popular but very dirty radio personality), seeing how much I could get away with, doing appearances in bars at night, staying out much too late, and just making it in to work every morning on a wing and a prayer.

Oh, I did just fine once the red light came on and I was broadcasting. No one ever knew I was doing the show on a couple of hours' sleep and a bunch of Tylenol. Others covered for me, staying past the end of their shift until I showed up, making excuses about what I did and said when I was doing appearances under the influence. I appreciated it at the time, but now I know that they were simply enabling a decadent lifestyle.

And it was a lifestyle I knew was not me. God whispered in my ear plenty during those times, but I was too proud, too vain, to hear it. There I was, trying to be a dad on weekends, then going back to show biz on Monday mornings. Living so large I often didn't know if it was night or day.

I went running out my door one afternoon, late for a remote broadcast, and almost ran over my neighbor, who was out cutting his lawn.

"Rick, slow down," he told me. "It's the PM!"

He had seen me make that mad dash for the car so many mornings, he figured I had my days and nights mixed up again.

That is why I almost made a big move when my old Spanish class buddy Bill Bussey called me one day with an offer. He had become partners in the ownership of a 50,000-watt AM station up in Jacksonville and wanted me to come be their morning personality. We had kept in touch after we ruined Mrs. Suco's life. Bill had started a radio network to carry Jacksonville State University sports, including the school's wildly successful football team. And by that time my dad was the head coach for the Gamecocks and had taken them to two Division II championship games.

I was sorely tempted to take the offer, mainly because of Bill. But the money they could offer was much less than K-98 was paying me, what with the commissions I was earning for selling advertising. It would have been back to the AM dial, too. However, it really wasn't the money or the dial position.

It was that things were going too well with the show by that time. People were listening, responding to the silliness I was doing on the air. I loved the freedom I had, even if I was charging off into sinful territory with many facets of the show.

Chaotic life or not, I didn't necessarily see Bill's offer as a door God was opening for me. As it turns out, that was exactly what it was. It was a door that would eventually lead in a totally different direction than I could have ever dreamed.

But first, it would take a national championship football game and a cell phone call from my mom from the 50-yard line to finally show me the way that He wanted me to go.

6 A Dark-Cloud Day

We may not understand why it has to be this way, but when God talks to us, He doesn't always make it perfectly clear what He is telling us to do. It requires faith sometimes, too, even if we understand perfectly what He is saying to us. When I get to heaven, I am going to walk right up to Abraham and Job and say, "Hi, fellers. I'm Bill 'Bubba' Bussey, and I want to talk to you guys about how God tests us sometimes."

Granted, He did not ask me to sacrifice my firstborn or plague me with an infestation of boils, but He did throw a high-hard-fastball test or two my way. I don't know if I wasn't listening hard enough or if God was speaking Spanish during those days—and we all know about me and

Spanish—but I was not receiving the message very loud and clear. Looking back, I can testify that all that happened made me so much stronger in so many ways, and especially in my faith. It also helped shape how the *Rick and Bubba Show* would eventually evolve.

But the Lord knows already that I had my doubts at the time. About whether or not the girl of my dreams would ever be Mrs. Bill "Bubba" Bussey. And how we were going to survive when all we had in the house to eat was thin-sliced bologna and day-old bread from the bakery outlet store.

I got my first paying radio job at the mighty AM 1280 WPID in Piedmont, Alabama. Oh, I must also admit that the folks at 92J let me be on the air from three to six on Christmas morning, or other equally glorious air shifts, and that I did it for free. Shoot, I would probably have paid them to allow me to be on their air! But the kind folks at WPID not only put me in the control room when some people could actually hear me—not very many—but they also paid me—not very much—to spin a mixture of Top 40 and country hits. Granted, it was Saturday afternoons and Sunday mornings on a station with limited coverage, but I was on the air, broadcasting, and I was getting paid for it.

It was at WPID that I first realized I could beg for food on the air and people would actually bring it to me. The owner of the station and a fellow announcer, Ted Allen, let me in on that little secret.

Someone called in and said, "The Goshen Volunteer Fire Department is having a fish fry today. Could you mention it on the radio?"

"Tell you what," I fired back. "If you'll bring me some hush puppies and some filets, I'll mention it several times and tell everybody how good it is."

And, miracle of miracles, they did!

Having a yard sale? Bring me a bowl of chili and I'll send you some buyers. Want to hear a song? Drop off some French fries and a cheeseburger and I'll play what you want to hear!

Of course, it wasn't all about being a deejay. I often worked Sunday afternoons, and that meant a continuous string of preachers who purchased blocks of time from the station. They would show up to do their shows, and I would have to take their money—cash only, because even preachers will bounce a check, you know—and give them a receipt. Only then was I supposed to allow them to go on the air at their allotted time. And it was up to me to cut them off when their half hour or hour was up, even if they were at the most emotional part of their sermons.

I admit that I sometimes prayed they wouldn't show up or have the cash to get on the air. Then I had some time to fill with records and I could be a deejay when the sun was actually up and people were awake and alert, potentially listening to their radios and WPID.

It finally occurred to me that driving to Piedmont for my big-time radio job was costing me more money than I was making, so I left that station. I had a side business doing car stereo installations, fixing televisions and CB radios, and installing satellite dishes, in addition to going to school.

Somewhere in the midst of all that, I was trying to maintain a social life, too, but nothing serious developed. All along there had been one young lady who kept making cameo appearances in my life. That was quite the story, too. Believe me: it is another example of God alternately testing and blessing me—all in His usual highly mysterious ways!

I have said before that it's one of life's great mysteries how Betty and I became husband and wife. I first met her when I was at Jacksonville High School. She was a student at nearby Pleasant Valley High. It was a typical complicated high school romantic entanglement that at first appeared to have no chance of ever working out. Praise the Lord, it did! Finally.

Hang on. This gets convoluted.

I was spending a great deal of time with a friend who was dating a girl from Pleasant Valley. His girlfriend, Sue Green, deduced that if she fixed me up with someone there at her school, she would get to see her boyfriend—my buddy—more often. She told me to pick any girl in the school who I might be interested in. Well, we were at a basketball game at the time, so I looked around and immediately chose the pretty, blonde cheerleader on the end of the line.

My friend's girlfriend winced. That cheerleader had had the same boyfriend since grade school. She told me to pick somebody else, so I chose Betty Walker, and Sue vowed to make it happen. While she was trying to work that miracle, I ran into Betty when I attended a beauty pageant at Pleasant Valley.

It was very difficult for me to *see* Betty and me together. No, I mean really difficult to see because I went to the pageant directly from an eye doctor appointment, and my eyes were still dilated. I was seeing everything through fuzz. I know she thought I was an odd person since

I was not able to focus on her, but I could make out enough to see how beautiful she was and to rekindle my interest in going out with her.

By the way, the judges liked her, too, because she won first runner-up in the beauty contest that night.

The matchmaker at Pleasant Valley finally convinced Betty to invite me to be her date for a school athletic banquet. A beautiful girl *and* a banquet? It just doesn't get any better than that. Where do I sign up?

Except there would be more hurdles to overcome. I had to mow the lawn the afternoon of the banquet, and I had to use my mother's old push mower. Remember those? You had to supply all the "push." It wore me out. I decided to take a quick nap so I would be fresh for my big first date with Betty and—you guessed it—I fell sound asleep and didn't wake up until ten that evening. Well, she was not very forgiving about the whole thing. It was clear to me that our relationship was over before it even started.

Then, several years later, I was in college at Jacksonville State, and I dropped by a blood donor drive that was being held on campus. Betty just happened to be there too. She seemed to have either forgotten the incident when I so rudely stood her up or she had decided to let bygones be bygones. Either way, she was even more gorgeous than I remembered.

She had just given blood and was coming outside when she saw me in line, waiting to go in. We talked a bit. I was thrilled that she seemed to no longer be holding a grudge against me for the nap incident, and we were having a nice visit. Suddenly she turned very pale and fainted dead away. I did the only thing I could do. I caught her.

Thankfully, she was okay, and I later enjoyed pointing out that she totally fell for me that day.

Still, it would be five more years before our paths crossed again, when I was helping out with a remote broadcast for the radio station at a video store. I was the salesperson and wasn't allowed to talk on the air.

We had a good crowd. Among them was Miss Betty Walker, who came over and said hello. We talked long enough for me to determine, to my dismay, that she had become engaged. That was some really bad news.

But she still suggested that I call her. She even wrote down her number on a slip of paper. Now, that was some really good news!

The number turned out to be bogus. Really bad news. Obviously, she was messing with me, finally getting even with me for my standing her up for the banquet.

It worked. I felt awful.

God, though, had one more coincidence waiting for me. A couple of weeks later, Betty got in touch with me. She was mad, all right. Mad that I hadn't called her as I had promised. When I explained about the bad number—and even hinted at my suspicions that she had given me a nonworking set of digits—she maintained she must have just written it down wrong, that she really wanted me to call. *Sure!* I thought.

To prove it, though, she suggested we go to a movie the next night. Again, I was skeptical. She would probably give me a bad address or have a bunch of big old Pleasant Valley boys waiting to beat me up. I suggested we meet at McDonald's. At least if she stood me up, I could have a Big Mac and some supersized French fries and the evening would not be a total loss. Assuming I still had all my teeth after what her big old buddies would do to me.

She did show, though, without henchmen, and we had a great time at the movie. You know how you have one of those dates where everything just goes right? Everything I said tickled her, and I knew by the end of the evening that I had fallen head over heels for her.

When I brought her back to her car, I don't know what made me do it, but I looked her right in the eyes and said, "I am going to marry you one day." She didn't punch me or tell me I was loopy or go screaming into the night to get away from this lunatic. She did proceed to break up with her fiancé, and we soon became a steady couple.

I was not home free yet, though. At one point, Betty decided we were moving too quickly and suggested we break up. I immediately decided to go into denial.

"It takes two people to go together and two people to break up," I told her without hesitation. "I will see you tomorrow." It was a calculated ploy, born out of desperation. Something told me that if I lost this woman again, I did not have any more coincidences left.

Amazingly, simply refusing to break up with her worked. We have now been married for more than twenty years and have two wonderful kids. I sometimes think about asking Betty if she would have really broken up with me if I had not refused to go along with the concept. I won't do it though. Knowing Betty, she would probably tell me the truth, and I might not want to hear it!

While all this was going on, I landed an unpaid internship at a local TV station, Channel 40, where I helped make commercials and learned more and more about what makes radio and TV work. My appetite for ownership and management pretty well matched the one for listener-supplied chili and cheeseburgers. Since I was on the job at the TV station during what amounted to off-hours for most normal folks who worked there, I had the chance to look through the broadcasting trade publications that were lying around. I even figured out a way to apply for some television station licenses that were coming available, and, wonder of wonders, I got them!

Of course, I didn't have the money to put any of them on the air, and the Federal Communications Commission, the government agency that regulates broadcasting, frowns on people who are awarded licenses and don't do anything with them. I did manage to sell them to folks who would be able to put a signal on those channels. I didn't make much money on the deal, but it stoked the fire to do more in broadcasting than be a deejay.

That was when God opened the door just a crack. He sent me Robin Mathis, a radio station owner from Mississippi, who had just put a brand-new 50,000-watt AM station on the air in my hometown of Jacksonville. Its big signal covered a lot of territory. It could conceivably be a genuine threat to the other AM stations in nearby Anniston and Gadsden, and even to the stations that penetrated the area all the way from Birmingham. Somehow I convinced Robin that this chubby, country-talking kid knew enough about radio that he was willing to hire me and make me the general manager of the station. Later he gave me the opportunity to buy in and become part owner, even though I had to leverage my limited finances to the max to do so.

It could have been that God was giving me enough rope to hang myself. I just didn't see it that way at the time. I know now He was opening the door just a little bit more, allowing me to peek inside, testing to see if I would come in with the right spirit.

Meanwhile Betty had finished nursing school and gotten a good registered nursing job—on her temporary license—at a local hospital. We never quite figured that she might not have the opportunity to pass her nursing boards before the required time or that her job would then revert to a patient care assistant, with a patient care assistant's pay rather than an RN's. Or that the station would have a tough time generating revenue with its adult contemporary format, competing with FMs playing basically the same music but in stereo with—as Steely Dan put it in their song "FM"—no static at all.

I saw none of this coming, though. I was having a blast. Never mind that the station's staff refused to let me go on the air, even if I was the boss, because of my accent and decidedly non–radio announcer's voice. I even had a sponsor who wanted me to record his commercial, but the staff rebelled. It hurt my feelings, but I gave in and let somebody else do it.

Once I was at the station, and as soon as I saw the need to try to attract a larger audience, my first call was to my old Spanish class buddy, Rick Burgess. By then he was on the air at K-98 FM in the Anniston/Oxford area, and he was easily the most popular thing on radio in east Alabama. I knew he was selling commercials, too, but we could make him the same deal. The only thing we couldn't do was come anywhere close to the salary and commissions he was making at K-98. Not at our AM station in tiny, little Jacksonville.

I made the pitch anyway. Rick was nice enough about it. but he turned us down cold. I respect him for that, though. I have learned from him that we should not sell ourselves short. Be realistic about what we are worth, what we bring to the table, and expect to be rewarded accordingly.

Well, Betty and I and my dream radio station were about to face some tough times. I knew we were in trouble when the power company showed up at our little house and threatened to pull the meter. That was when I went to my mother and borrowed enough money to keep the lights on.

We were doing all we could to make the station work, but it just was not happening. The stress was taking a toll on me. I thought I was going to have a heart attack, so I booked an appointment with a doctor, something I almost never did. It was on the way to that appointment that something or someone spoke to me. The message this time was as clear as our 50,000-watt radio signal.

We had to change the format of WJXL to contemporary Christian music. At that time there were few full-time all-Christian stations, and I was convinced we could meet a need. Besides, it had to be God leading us that way. How could it not work?

But it meant giving up some of our biggest sources of revenue: beer and nightclubs.

The format might have worked given some time, or if we had not been so far down that it was difficult to recover. I couldn't see a way out, but I was determined to avoid bankruptcy. It was just not an option that I wanted to consider. I couldn't stand the thought of anyone we legitimately owed money not getting all they were entitled to. And I desperately wanted to justify the confidence Robin Mathis showed in me when he hired me. We scratched and clawed, prayed and worked. And I had some real heart-to-hearts with God.

What are You telling me? I asked Him.

I was trying to be a growing Christian, the way my parents had taught me. I read my Bible. I went to church. I tithed even when it meant slicing the bologna thinner still. I had even changed the format of my station to contemporary Christian music. What else could He want from me?

That was when the power company came and pulled the meter at the transmitter. We were off the air, what broadcasters—even in radio—call "going dark." I couldn't see that all this was the door opening a little wider, inviting me to take the next step to what would eventually be His plan for us. All I saw was a dark-cloud day.

That was when an old friend, Rob Rosson, called me up and asked if I was interested in a job at the TV station where he worked, Channel 44 in Gadsden. Well, the radio station was off the air while we struggled to find a buyer, so I was thinking a job was not a bad idea at the time.

The truth is, I was convinced that God's door had already slammed shut in my face!

It was a sales job at the TV station, not engineering, and not at all what I wanted to do. I would be selling commercials on a secular station, including for some clients who were definitely selling commercials to some sponsors I was not comfortable with. I even had concerns about some of the programming we had on the air at the time. But our little answering machine at home was full every night with calls from bill collectors. My mother provided the final push I needed.

"Bill, if God is leading you down a path, and if this is the only way He is showing you, it may just be the right path for you," she said. There was something in there about not trying to guess what God had in mind but just to follow and trust Him. She talked about Daniel, facing adversity, yet refusing to compromise. "Compromise will bring you fire, just like it did Daniel," she told me. Her words made good sense to me, especially while I was playing back those threatening messages from creditors on the answering machine each evening.

I took the job at Channel 44, even though I almost fainted when I saw the dollar amount of advertising I was expected to sell. Expected to sell on a station with little or no ratings. But then, out of the blue, I had the opportunity to pitch InTouch Ministries, the television arm of Dr. Charles Stanley, a pastor in Atlanta, trying to convince them to put their television show on our station.

I must have said the right things, because I made the sale and it was the biggest sale the station had ever had. That one account reached my sales goal for the entire year! Everything else would be gravy. And I do love gravy! Maybe I could even take some time off to find a serious buyer for WJXL before that anchor dragged us down.

As it usually does in the fast-paced world of broadcasting, though, change came quickly. The TV station decided to go a different direction. The owners immediately cut back on the number of employees, including those who were making too much money on accounts that were already on the air and did not have to be resold or serviced. Just when it appeared we were getting our heads above water, Betty and I were drowning again.

I didn't even call Betty to tell her the news. I started home from Gadsden and got to the bridge that crosses the Coosa River. I confess the fleshly side of me allowed into my brain a fleeting thought about steering a little to the right and going straight into those swirling, muddy waters. Thankfully my spiritual side won out, giving me the peace to drive on.

Then, as it inevitably does with us fat folks, hunger overcame any other emotions I might have been feeling at the time. I turned into a restaurant parking lot. Telling Betty this latest development, plotting our next move, trying to figure out why God kept slamming the door in our faces—all that would have to wait until I could get some fried chicken and biscuits and gravy. Biscuits and gravy can heal anything.

I had just ordered and sat down when someone came over and tapped me on the shoulder. It was Jimmy Vineyard, the general manager of Q104, the legendary radio station in Gadsden. The station had fallen on hard times in the last few years, and Jimmy had been brought in by its owners to try to fix it. I had done a little bit of part-time engineering, and the TV station and the Q shared the same tower, so we knew each other. I was surprised, though, that he knew so much about me.

"Hey, congratulations on the big sale," he told me. Word had gotten out about that InTouch Ministries thing, I guess. "I've been meaning to call you and see if you know of anybody I could hire to come engineer the Q. My guy has gone to a station in Birmingham, and I need somebody in a hurry."

I almost choked on my drink.

I didn't share the story of my recent career redirection, but I told Jimmy that I had been thinking about getting back into engineering, losing the coat and tie, getting my hands dirty again. He made me the job offer right there. And before my chicken and biscuits even showed up, I accepted it.

Since I was always a gimmick guy, I had one of the first cellular telephones, a thing about the size and approximate weight of a cement block. When I got back in the car, I dialed up Betty as I passed the spot where, only an hour before, I had a quick thought of plunging my car into the Coosa River.

"Honey, I've got bad news and I've got some really good news," I told her.

It had to be God. It had to be Him who led me to the fried chicken restaurant that day and the chance meeting with Jimmy Vineyard. Just when Betty and I were at our lowest point, just when we were questioning Him and His plan for us, just when I was contemplating slamming the door He was opening, He put me in exactly the right spot at exactly the right time.

How fitting that it was over a plate of fried chicken, biscuits, and gravy! God is good!

Of course, I had no way of knowing that the Lord was nowhere close to finished with me. He was about to steer another radio guy in my direction again, and His plan for Rick and Bubba would finally be back on track.

On track, maybe, but not before He showed me a few more rough stretches of rail!

7 "If You Had Come to Work for Us ..."

I—Rick—don't believe in coincidences. I believe God does things for a reason. We are not supposed to question His thinking, but believe me when I tell you that I have done some really, really hard thinking about why some things have happened the way they did.

What if my dad had not taken the Jacksonville State Gamecocks to his third national championship game?

What if Bubba had not been there at the game with that cell phone the size of a cement block?

What if my boss had not made me do a remote broadcast that day?

In my mind, I had the world by the tail in a downhill drag. I was doing shock-jock morning radio on FM. Everyplace I went in the area, people knew my name and about my anti–country music stance and all the other off-the-wall things I did on my radio show. I was picking up extra money—pretty good money for such a small market—selling commercials and doing remote broadcasts and beer company promotions in clubs, where I probably would have hung out for free even if I wasn't getting paid to be there.

Did I mention that it was all a blur? That I knew at some level I was not living the life I knew I should be living? Doing things my mom and dad would not have been proud of? Things I was not proud of? Things I would not have wanted my two kids to know I was doing?

But I was sure proud of my dad. He had left Oxford High School to become the head football coach at Jacksonville State University. He was immediately successful there and took the team to a pair of Division II college football championship games. He didn't win either one of those games, but it was still a remarkable feat for a team from a tiny school in east Alabama that played in the shadows of Southeastern Conference schools like Auburn, Alabama, and Georgia.

My old buddy Bill Bussey had been busy, first with ownership of his station and then as engineer at Q104, but he somehow found the time to create a radio network of stations to carry the Jax State games. Even though I usually had to work on Saturday afternoons—prime time for radio remote broadcasts—I could still listen to those games on the network and keep up with Dad and the Gamecocks. I spent many days at some remote at a used car lot somewhere with one earphone on one ear, waiting for my cue to talk, and another earphone on my other ear, listening to the play-by-play of the game on Bill's network, silently cheering on my dad and my old school.

After Bill became the chief engineer at Q104 in Gadsden, he called me up one day and asked if I was interested in coming over and being the station's morning personality. Well, I had to think about it for a bit.

The Q had once been a powerhouse in the broad area of Alabama and Georgia between Birmingham and Atlanta. The station had fallen on hard times, though, and lost much of its luster. And its audience too. The truth is, despite my anti–country music efforts, the big country stations were kicking the Q's hind end. The station was operating at reduced power because there was not enough money to fix some technical issues. They had suffered through several sets of undercapitalized owners, and things had deteriorated greatly. Bill told me the latest owners had big plans for the Q. They were in the process of fixing all that was broken, hiring a good staff, and bringing the station back to its former glory.

Still, the money they were offering me to come over and do mornings was less than what I was making in Anniston/Oxford, never mind that I was working eighteen-hour days plus weekends to earn it. Between the show, selling commercials, hosting remotes, and doing all those paid nightclub appearances, I thought I was in high cotton.

Besides, I felt some loyalty to the owners at K-98. They hired me and assured me they would let me do what I wanted to do on the air, and I promised I would work hard to build them an audience and make them money. I know they cringed sometimes when they heard what I did when I turned on that microphone, but they kept their promise. I felt like I should keep mine too.

Oh, I suppose there were job offers that would have lured me away—a chance to work with the legendary Mark and Brian at I-95 in Birmingham or some big-market gig that paid four or five times what I was making at K-98. I wasn't dumb, and I did have two kids to help support by then. But I still had reservations about making a move to the Q. And there was that pesky thing about loyalty to my present employer. I have never been one to jump from job to job.

I told Bill how much I appreciated the chance, that I was flattered they were interested in me, but I turned down the Q and kept burning the candle at both ends at K-98.

As head coach at Jacksonville State University, my dad won fifty-six games in five years and was ultimately headed to his team's third Division II championship game. That was truly amazing, but there was one more subplot. Because of their success in football under my dad, the school's board of directors had decided to take the football program up a very big step toward the big time, to the highly competitive Division I-AA. My dad let everyone know what a bad decision he thought that was, that a school like Jacksonville State had no business trying to compete there. It was difficult enough to do what they had done in Division II. He knew they were about to become a victim of their own success, and he told them so. Nobody listened to him. The deal was done.

As it turned out, this would almost certainly be Jacksonville State's final shot at a national championship, at least for a long, long time. Furthermore, that would probably make it my dad's last hurrah as well. I knew how much winning that final championship game would mean to him. There was no way I was going to miss it.

One problem. It was going to be on a Saturday—prime time for radio remote broadcasts—and Old Rick was king of the radio remotes.

I planned weeks in advance to be sure I did not have a remote broadcast the day of the championship game in case the team made it that far. I wanted desperately to be there to help cheer him and the Gamecocks on.

One morning, the week of the championship, my boss at the radio station came to me and announced he had sold a remote broadcast for Saturday. That Saturday. It was to be from the location of one of the station's biggest sponsors, and the broadcast was scheduled to take place at the exact time of my dad's big game.

"Man, I was planning on going to the game," I told him. "Could you talk to the client and see if someone else could do the remote?"

I pointed out that most people in our area would be either at the game or be listening to it on the radio anyway—not listening to Rick Burgess doing four live cut-ins per hour for three hours. It was a terrible idea to do a remote at that time.

The manager scratched his head and hemmed and hawed around for a bit. He told me the store's owner really wanted me and nobody else, that the sponsor was, after all, one of our biggest accounts, and that the customer is always right. But he finally and reluctantly told me that he would go back and ask the owner if it would be okay for someone else to do the broadcast this time, that we would make it up to him somehow.

I knew the store's owner, and I had no doubt he would accept someone else doing the remote this one time. I made my plans to go to the big game and witness my dad's crowning achievement.

My boss called me aside the next day just as I was getting off the air.

"Rick, I'm sorry. I asked them and they said they had to have you or they wouldn't even do the remote. We need the revenue."

My heart fell. As I said before, I was—and am—a loyal son of a gun. My dad had instilled such a strong work ethic in me that it never occurred to me to tell the manager what he could do with his stinking remote broadcast. I just swallowed hard, stomped out the door, and made sure I had fresh batteries in my little portable radio so I could listen to the game while I did the remote.

When I walked into the store that Saturday afternoon to set up, the owner looked at me wide-eyed. He was clearly surprised to see me there.

"What in the world are you doing here, Rick?" he asked. "I figured you would be at the championship game."

That's when it hit me. The station manager had lied to me. The sponsor had never asked for me specifically in the first place. Of if he had, my boss was too timid to ask the sponsor for a change in talent for the remote. The manager thought so little of me that he never made the request, even knowing what the game meant to me.

I don't ever remember being as mad as I was that day. Picture "livid." That was what I was. Livid. But mad as I was, I did one heck of a remote broadcast, giving the sponsor more than his money's worth. That's just the way I am.

I listened to the game when I could, secretly cheering every great play that I was able to hear, hurting when things went against the

Gamecocks, picturing my mom in the stands with my brother and sister, my dad pacing the sidelines, the team giving it their all, the crowd going berserk, the band playing the fight song. Some of the people who came by the remote broadcast that day probably thought the big guy with the two sets of headphones on his head was having some kind of conniption fit the way I was pacing, cheering, fussing, and crying.

The Gamecocks won, and my dad finally got his national championship.

Okay, I cried, and I didn't care who saw me. Cried not because I wasn't there with my family, but because I was so proud of Dad and the team and everyone else—including my mom, by the way, who was responsible for what they had accomplished. I knew how hard all of them had worked for this moment and how it was so worth it when they ultimately won it all.

Then I went back to selling stuff on the radio, giving away free balloons and hot dogs for the kids, a T-shirt for the next customer who walked in the door, and "Stop by for the Gamecock national championship special prices, this afternoon only during the big K-98 remote broadcast with Rick Burgess here."

Not long after the game had ended and I'd gotten back home, the telephone rang.

"Hello?"

"Rick, Bill Bussey. I got somebody here who wants to talk to you."

He put my mother on his cell phone so she could tell me about how the game had gone, to give me the highlights of how we had done it. At that very moment, she was standing on the 50-yard line at the stadium, right in the middle of the wild and glorious celebration.

It seems that she, with the help of Gamecock broadcast color commentator Ray Hammett, had located a fellow in the crowd who was toting around a big old cellular telephone. She asked him if she could use it to make a very important call.

At first Bill hadn't known who this excited woman was, asking to use his telephone, but then she introduced herself as Coach Burgess's wife.

"I'm Bill Bussey. A friend of Rick's. By the way, where is Rick?" he asked her, looking around in the melee on the field to try to spot me.

"He had to work. A remote broadcast or something."

I cried some more as I talked to my mother and told her to give Dad a big hug for me until I could do it in person. She agreed to do so, told me she loved me and that she wished I could have been there, and then she handed the phone back to Bill.

"Rick, what in the world are you doing?"

"Remote broadcast. You know, the show must go on or something like that."

There was a moment of silence then, with just the whoops and yells of the excited crowd in the background and the Gamecock band playing the fight song yet again, but now with even more feeling.

"You know something? If you had come to work at the Q, you would be standing here at the 50-yard line right now with your mom and me."

Those simple words hit home. Hit home so hard it almost knocked the breath out of me.

I turned in my notice on Monday and worked out my two weeks on K-98. I gave them some great shows during those two weeks, too, before I left and made the move over to the Q.

You see, even a bonehead like me had figured out that when God was trying to tell me something, I should probably pay closer attention.

8 Shakespeare's Worst Nightmare

I—Bubba—would love to tell everyone that the *Rick and Bubba Show* was a coolly calculated move, based on solid planning and expensive audience research. I would like to say that Rick Burgess and I knew from the day he went on the air at the Q that we would soon be partners on the airwaves, and that the two-man show we cobbled together would eventually be the number one radio program in the area and nationally syndicated with hundreds of thousands of loyal listeners.

I'd love to do that, but I don't lie.

Of course, I would also be thrilled to tell you that we knew all along it was the hand of God that put us in that cramped little studio together, reading Shakespeare quotes and urging listeners to give "Rick and Bubba" shout-outs on other people's radio stations. I thank Him for it every day now, but I know neither of us saw at the time what He had in store for us.

Truth is, neither did the people we worked for. And that led to some very interesting times. Or, as our old friend Bill Shakespeare said in act 1, scene 2 of *Julius Caesar*—who, by the way, makes a very good salad, but go ahead and pay extra for the baby shrimp:

Men at some time are masters of their fates;
The fault, dear Brutus, is not in our stars,
But in ourselves.

Maybe I wasn't playing fair when I reminded Rick that he could have been at the big game that day—had he accepted my invitation to finally come to a station where I worked. I do understand why he kept turning me down, and I have learned a lot from the way he handles things like this.

It worked, though, didn't it?

Rick was immediately the best thing on the station, but between our weak signal and the lack of promotion and the strength of the high-powered country music stations on either side of us on the dial, the Q was still having a tough time staying afloat. Our general manager, Jimmy Vineyard, the visionary who hired me in the first place, had already moved on to bigger things. Our new boss, Mark Bass, had his hands full. Commercials on the station were selling for ten bucks each, which wouldn't generate enough revenue to pay the power bill.

Mark had inherited a mess. That included a loud, long-haired, sweat-pants-wearing morning show host and an engineer who still harbored a dream of being on the air.

While we had our moments with Mark, we have to acknowledge that he taught us much of what we know about guerrilla marketing, about getting the most promotion for the least amount of money. We quickly nicknamed Mark Bass "the Hammer." That was because he always urged us to go full force, hammer down.

"Take the fight to them!" he counseled us.

God put him there for a purpose, the right man at the right time. I can't imagine anybody else running a radio station anywhere in America who would have allowed Rick and me to get together and do the kind of show we did.

After he had been on the air on the Q for a few weeks, Rick called me into the studio one morning during his show to ask if we were having trouble with the telephones. He would try to do a giveaway on the air and nobody—*nobody*—called in to win. He would make up the name of a winner and act like the phones were jangling off the hook.

It didn't take Rick long to realize that if he was going to build a following, he was going to have to throw away the radio rulebook.

See, radio and those who run it have a rather narrow idea of what should and should not be done on the air. Research-loving program directors and radio consultant goobs maintain that the stations must be "vanilla," that nothing occur on the airwaves that might shock or create the risk of chasing off listeners.

"Personalities"—if you really want to use that term—have to play music, and it must be music that fits the "format." And the "safer" the music is, the less risk that someone might tune out. They have done a wonderful job of removing any spontaneity, creativity, or just plain fun from radio, all in the name of being "safe." In the process they have turned a powerful, personal medium into bland and boring background noise.

Can you tell how I feel about this subject?

Partly out of desperation, but partly because of his own instincts, Rick started improvising with his *Morning Extravaganza*. Much to the dismay of the program director and general manager, he began talking more and not playing all the songs that the music log told him to play. And when he talked, he stopped using the fake "deejay voice" that everyone else employed. He talked like a regular person, which at that time was a radical concept.

He did something else, too, that went against all that was holy in the staid and formatted world of broadcasting. Since the phones appeared to be dead and he couldn't interact with listeners that way, he began putting on the air some of the other people who worked at the station. Dave Fitz was a longtime well-respected newsman who did recorded newscasts on the Q and live ones on her sister AM station, WAAX. His deep voice and straight delivery put a serious tone on every story he read. Rick began to mimic his dulcet tones and then bring Dave into the studio to pick at him some more. It wasn't done in a mean way, but it was funny as all get-out. We still maintain that we ruined Dave's twenty-year reputation as a journalist in only a few weeks.

Later the station hired a young lady named Sherri Bodine to do news. Rick immediately made her a part of the show, with a bit about how he had fallen for her and would one day make her his wife. That live on-the-air stalking became a running theme on the show, backed up with Eric Clapton's "Wonderful Tonight" as a soundtrack.

Rick and I went to lunch almost every day after he got off the air. (It is still amazing to me how many good things happen over lunch, so let that be a lesson to you dieters out there!) To neither of our surprise, we fell right back into the off-the-cuff comedy routine we originally debuted in Mrs. Suco's Spanish class at Jax State, and we kept folks around our table at the local buffet restaurant well entertained. They got a meal and a show for their $5.99!

I also came up with lots of ideas for the show. Inevitably Rick asked me to start coming into the studio and doing stuff on the show, figuring we could bring the same material that we created over the salad bar to the airwaves at the Q. Because of my drawl, he nicknamed me "Uncle Bubba." Everybody in Alabama had an Uncle Bubba, and he sounded just like Bill Bussey, he told me.

The first day I made my appearance on the Q, I wasn't really nervous. I had been on the air many times, but I always had records to play and had no pressure to try to be funny. I had no idea what I was going to do, and I admit my mind was a blank as I sat down at the other microphone I had wired into the control board.

We had talked about an idea in which Rick would read a quote from a play by William Shakespeare, and listeners were supposed to call in and guess the play it came from. This came from a book of radio show ideas—something written for deejays by some consultant somewhere. It was probably the same guy who thought reading celebrity birthdays and daily horoscopes on the air was the height of radio entertainment.

Anyway, Rick thought it would be funny if he read it in a deep, Southern drawl and otherwise treated it like a serious contest.

William Shakespeare read by a redneck. It did have its comedic possibilities, I agreed.

But just as he was getting ready to do the bit, it suddenly occurred to Rick that if he wanted the Bard read in a Southern accent, he had one of radio's best, right there across the console from him.

"It would be funnier if you read it, Bill," he told me.

Then I heard some dramatic music playing in my headphones and Rick telling the audience that Uncle Bubba was going to "feed the beast," that I would read aloud a quote from Shakespeare. The first listener to call in and guess the play from which it came would win a free oil change or something of equally immense value. In my best east Alabama accent, I completely butchered the King's English, the immortal words of history's greatest playwright, right there in front of—well—dozens of listeners.

We actually got calls, though. Calls from people who had probably paid as much attention back in high school literature class as Rick and I did, but they ventured guesses anyway. We ad-libbed around the names of the plays: "*Henry IV*, the nurse's favorite," "*Macbeth*? No, that's mac-wrong, but thanks for mac-trying," and more.

Well, Rick and I and the few folks who were listening thought it was about the funniest dang thing ever to be broadcast on the radio. We quickly dubbed it "Good Old Boy Theater" and added a grand buildup to the simple little contest, all to make it even sillier. I had stepped in and done the bit a couple of times a week for two weeks when Mark Bass took Rick aside.

"You should stop having Bill Bussey on the air," he told Rick, point-blank.

"Why?" he asked.

"You are our morning man. Bill is the engineer."

The truth is, Mark was afraid he was going to lose his station engineer, and it was hard to find them in towns like Gadsden.

Mark had noticed that I was spending more and more time sitting in on the show. Before long I was doing much more with Rick than simply reading the Bard in a thick Southern accent. I began finding excuses to be at the station early, just so I could pop into the studio and be on Rick's show. Rick was astute enough to realize that his program was much stronger when he had someone to bounce off of. Listener calls were picking up some, but they were still few and far between. Rick was catching grief, too, for involving the newspeople, who were supposed to be above all the hilarity of the *Extravaganza*.

Who better than Uncle Bubba to be an occasional character?

I told Rick I didn't think I could be funny more than a couple of times a week. Rick reminds me often that I am still living up to that.

Again, I give full credit to Rick for deciding I needed to be more than a recurring character. He saw that we had chemistry, that the sum of what we did together was much greater than each of us alone. But as sure as I was about the potential of a two-man show, it was Rick who was convinced enough to do something about it. He marched into the general manager's office and told him that we needed to do the *Rick and Bubba Show*, and to do that, he needed Bubba.

You would have thought Rick was proposing putting on the air for four hours a day the sound of fingernails clawing a chalkboard.

Mark had dozens of good reasons why it wouldn't work. The main one was basic. He wanted me to engineer and Rick to do the radio show. Oh, he liked "Good Old Boy Theater" better once a salesman sold a sponsor for it, but he still didn't want me to cohost a show with Rick.

So that was it. I was ready to surrender, to go in and do my thing a few times a week and reserve the rest of our act for our audience at the buffet restaurant. Besides, I finally had a pretty good job as chief engineer, making more money than most people in my family had ever made.

"The Rick and Bubba Show." It did have a nice sound to it. But if the Lord didn't want it to happen, I would just have to live with it.

If somebody is standing in the middle of a railroad track and a train is bearing down on him, he could take the attitude that "if it is God's will that this train won't kill me, He will derail the train."

Or he could figure that God gave him the ability and the common sense to jump off the track.

It was Rick Burgess who got us both off the track.

Or on track, depending on how you look at it.

9 Fat Chat

You want to know what I—Rick—am thankful for? I am thankful for the Q and for God leading me there. If not for that dumpy little radio station, right there behind the skating rink on the banks of the mighty Coosa River, I would not have teamed up with Bill "Bubba" Bussey and became half of the *Rick and Bubba Show*. I doubt I would have met Miss Sherri Bodine or had the opportunity to make her my wife, either. That's a miracle in itself.

I might well have stayed on the chaotic path I had embarked upon back in Anniston, with the clubs, the drinking, the lifestyle. Once Bill and I teamed up, however, and once I made Sherri realize I was not just the mullet-wearing wild man I appeared to be, everything just felt right all of a sudden.

Oh, we had many challenges to overcome, but in late 1993 and early 1994, I felt a peace come over me that I have trouble explaining to people. If anything, I was living an even more frenetic life. Bill and I were going ninety-to-nothing, trying to build the show with no money or help. There were plenty of opportunities to just shut it down and go get a real job. Even when we proved our point and the show was validated by financial and ratings success, very few people in the radio business believed in it, including the ones who gave us our jobs and had the power to put our little radio show right out on the street.

But something made us keep pushing.

Something? *Somebody*. And I thank Him for it every single day.

We knew the show would work. It already was. The phones lit up when Bill was in the studio with me. People stopped us on the street and told us how much they liked what we were doing. I knew getting Bill on full-time was just the first step. I had been doing a lot of thinking, and I figured I knew exactly what direction to take the show. It would be radical, compared to what the country stations were doing, but I knew it would work. Or I would die trying.

Mark remained opposed to the idea of bringing on Bill as a major part of the show. "We hired you, Rick, to do our morning show," he told me. "So do it. I hired Bussey to be the engineer. Let him engineer. I'd end up losing an engineer and messing up our morning show at the same time."

He had a point about losing an engineer. It was hard to find those guys in small markets, and since we were running the station on a shoestring, it took a special guy to keep us on the air with spit and baling wire. But I expected this argument, and I had an ace up my sleeve.

"I understand, Boss. But here's what I'm willing to do. I will take a three-thousand-dollar pay cut so you can pay a part-time engineer to help Bill. That would free him up to be on the show every day."

Look, I needed the three thousand bucks, but I was so sure we could do a great show—and that it would be the most fun I had ever had on the air, even if it flopped—that I was willing to make that investment in the concept.

Mark was taken aback. Nobody had ever pulled that trick on him before. He didn't know how to respond, other than to agree to my deal. And to his credit, once he bought into the idea of our very unconventional two-man show, Mark taught us a lot.

So it was that in January 1994, the *Rick and Bubba Show* was unleashed. I wish I could tell you I foresaw what was about to happen, how wild and woolly our lives were about to be, but I didn't.

So many things were perfectly clear to me, though. It was as if someone were whispering in my ear, telling me what to do and what not to do. I was already losing that fake voice most radio announcers used. I no longer read the full weather forecast, including wind speed and direction, and I ignored what we call "liner cards," the little scripted announcements and slogans we were supposed to read between records.

Records? I had developed the idea that a music-formatted radio station was limited by the music it played. If a listener didn't like rap or rock, he wouldn't listen to the station just to hear the personality, no matter how entertaining he or she was between the records the listener hated. We began playing fewer and fewer records, talking more and more, involving listeners and, as always, other people around the station, talking about them and what was going on in their lives.

See, I had come to a realization one Sunday afternoon while attending a family get-together at my folks' house. We were all out on the deck, talking, laughing, having a great time as we usually did when we all got together. We were not trying to entertain each other or make one another laugh, but I noticed that the funniest stuff, the most engaging, was what was real.

Bill and I began bringing stories from our own lives to the show, things I did with my kids, funny things that happened at the drive-through, something we saw while out doing an appearance at a station event. My on-air wooing of Miss Sherri Bodine became a regular soap opera on the show, even though in real life, it seemed to be going nowhere. People came up to me all the time to urge me to keep pursuing her, that she would eventually see the light.

We had decided, consciously or not, to be real on the radio. Not to manufacture personalities to suit some consultant's or corporate program director's view of what made great radio. We didn't do pre-recorded or scripted comedy bits with a laugh track and fake guffaws to show listeners where they were supposed to laugh. And no celebrity birthdays or horoscopes! We made fun of the other stations that did all this old, hackneyed junk, and that attitude struck a chord with our listeners. They were as bored with all that stuff as we were.

We became an anti-radio radio show, and people loved it.

Finally, we decided to take it to the next level. We heard—and talked about on the air—that the big-station program directors in Birmingham were saying that Bill and I talked too much, that not only were we two rubes on the air but we were a couple of chatty rubes. Well, between you and me, we were thrilled they even knew who we were and that we had created enough of a bump in the ratings down there with our weak little signal and un-radio radio show that they even acknowledged our existence. I doubt they really worried much about us at that point, but we sure took it as a compliment. We got on the air and made a big deal out of it and proclaimed that we would become even chattier. We would stop playing music at all on Fridays. And we would play on our redneckism and obesity.

"Fat Chat" was born. And we had become the "two sexiest fat men alive." We even started looking for a toll-free telephone number and would eventually get 877-WE BE BIG.

I admit—and I think Bill will too—that when we came to the end of that first four-hour Friday show without records, we were a couple of tired fat boys. We were mentally drained, whipped! I'm not even sure we wanted to continue doing music-free Fridays after that first one.

But the reaction was amazing. We couldn't have gone back to playing songs if we'd wanted to. The listeners wouldn't have allowed it.

I came to realize something else, and this was way too profound for me to have thought of on my own. A higher power was already working mightily.

Despite not having any money to promote our show and the

station, and regardless of the fact that the station had a marginal signal in many of the places where people lived, and even though we were competing against radio stations with highly paid programming consultants, lots of money for promotional billboards and station vans, and high-dollar contests, Bill and I actually had a huge advantage over those other guys.

We had none of what they had, but we had something they didn't.

See, those stations were, in effect, working in a box. Their formats and their consultant-based programming had them roped in. They were sorely limited in what they could and would do to repel a good, creative, hardworking competitor. They didn't know how to counter what we were doing.

Rick and Bubba have launched many acts at Fat Fest and Turkey Toss. Pictured here with Zac Brown Band

First, there was no way they could outwork us. There was that strong work ethic Bill and I have talked about. We were hungry. We knew we were right about what we were doing because the listeners told us so. You could feel it growing, and we did not get cocky and lie down on the job. We still haven't and never will.

I know there are others out there who would love to knock off the Rick and Bubba Show, and are just as desperately driven to do it as Bill and I were in 1994. Still, they will have to outwork us if they hope to have a chance.

And there was something else. They had no way of anticipating what we were willing to do next so long as we kept breaking all the rules of radio broadcasting. We were not beholden to a consultant or some suit at corporate headquarters. We could come up with an idea over lunch and have it on the air the next day. Or even better, just turn on our microphones and do something totally outrageous. Something real that did not come out of a consultant's guidebook or as the result of a research project.

Their answer? Play more of the best of the '70s, '80s, and '90s. Play the best mix of your favorites. Offer more and better country with less talk. All radio goob reactions! We knew that they couldn't come up with anything different and that this was the number one reason they wouldn't be able to fight back.

We also knew we had to create our own promotion, to generate some buzz and awareness to attract new listeners to the show. We were confident that word of mouth would eventually work, but we knew it took time. We were not sure how much time our owners would give us to become a rollicking success.

Mark Bass helped with motivation and ideas. The rest we just made up on the fly.

Since we had no station van, we took Bill's old clunker of a car and painted it up with shoe polish. Then we did the same with an ancient van I had inherited from somewhere. Never mind that it hardly ran and left a cloud of blue smoke everywhere it went. It didn't even have a reverse gear until we convinced the station manager to do a trade with an automatic transmission place. Finally we could park it somewhere without a turnaround.

That old, rusty van became the "Rick and Bubba Funmobile," the first in a long line of unimpressive but funny vehicles. Ugly or not, it was instantly recognizable wherever we went and is still legendary among the early adopters of the show.

We also came to realize something very basic about radio: station loyalty was quickly going away as big conglomerates were buying more and more stations. Those guys tended to manage radio stations as if they were fast-food restaurants, running them cheap, trying to pump up cash flow so they could sell them quickly and for a profit. All that so their publicly held companies could hit some kind of quarterly profit number they had guaranteed Wall Street.

That meant they needed to keep costs down while they reduced what they considered risks to a minimum. That included personalities. They replaced their on-air programming with "safe," highly researched music formats. Personalities tended to sometimes take sick days, to want vacations, to ask for more money. Or they jumped to other stations if they built up a following. All of that created uncertainty, something that could not be tolerated.

So these owners put deep-voiced but dull "nonoffensive" announcers on the air, piped in from Dallas or Miami, reading the same liner cards for Gadsden or Birmingham as they were for Seattle or Boise. Or they went the other direction entirely and took syndicated shock jocks who were on the air in the big cities, and put their vile form of humor on the air in their towns. They never considered how those type shows would play in Jackson or Tallahassee or Birmingham. They were cheap. They had audiences in Miami or New York. Put them on the air in Chattanooga and stand back and see what happens.

We knew that people did not really care about the station or the slogans anymore, or even so much about the music they played. They were loyal to personalities they liked, who made them laugh or feel good, even when things might not be going so great in their everyday lives. There was no danger to us in taking on the big stations, poking fun at them and their boring programming. Or even giving them grief about their big promotions.

The first example of that came with Sand Mountain Sam. The number one station in the area—a country music station, of course, which broadcast from a town atop Sand Mountain in east Alabama—did an annual promotion around Groundhog Day. In an amazing display of creativity for them, they employed an opossum—the official roadkill animal of Alabama—as the local shadow-watcher, determining the amount of winter weather we had left each February.

We saw our chance to really get under their skin and have some fun too. Bubba and I went on the air, claiming we had gotten word from an anonymous source at the station that they were torturing the poor marsupial, just for the sake of this promotion. We also passed along the intel that the pitiful possum would be killed once the event was over. We created a huge backlash of animal lovers, upset about the treatment of some poor critter, all in the name of trying to build ratings on a radio station.

We printed up "Save Sand Mountain Sam" T-shirts with our caricatures on them and then sold them for a nice profit. Our entrepreneurial gene had become suddenly dominant, and we have been selling shirts and caps—for a profit—ever since.

The possum promotion was a huge success. People knew it was all tongue-in-cheek, that we were just making fun of the other station, but they loved it.

With success comes power. The groundswell was obvious and the ratings were growing. Our salespeople were taking orders for commercials from sponsors left and right. Even the reluctant station manager was suddenly our biggest fan. That meant nothing was off-limits, that we had a longer leash, and we took advantage of that, you can be sure.

We did a station promotion where listeners were to go by sponsor locations and register for a free trip to Los Angeles, accompanied by the two fat boys, Rick and Bubba. As it turns out, the winner's name was pulled from a registration box that a salesperson had placed at a pawnshop. The winner was—how do I put this nicely?—a character. So was her pistol-toting, beer-swigging boyfriend. Our adventures with Wanda and her boyfriend, Willy, became a classic, and the telling of that story is one of the more popular tracks on one of our "Best of . . ." CDs. The whole sad tale gets played often when Bill and I are on vacation and we do "best of" request shows. ("Willie and Wanda"

Rick and Bubba backstage at the GMAs with Toby Mac

and Bubba's encounter with a drunken midget at a Foreigner concert are neck-and-neck number one most-requested segments on our "best of" shows.)

But on that trip we decided to take advantage of being on the West Coast to try to visit with a couple of our radio heroes, Mark Thompson and Brian Phelps. They were former Birmingham radio personalities who were hired away and quickly made it big in LA. Theirs was one of the first radio shows we knew about that did outrageous, out-of-studio stunts and the kind of creative and fun things the typical owners and consultants and program directors hated. They had been a genesis for where we had taken our own show.

To our surprise they acted as if they knew who we were. Friends back in Birmingham had already told them about the two sexiest fat men alive and what we were doing out there in the boondocks to shake up that whole end of the radio dial. They enthusiastically invited us to come down to KLOS and hang out with them after they got off the air. I shouldn't have been surprised that they turned out to be just two regular guys and really seemed to get what we were trying to do. We even took time to play some basketball on a court they had built behind the station. We thought that was the coolest thing ever!

But the big thing was, both of them assured us that we were on the right track—listeners would respond to people who were "real" on the radio, radio people the average listener could identify with. Their encouragement meant a lot to us, and despite our frustrations with Willy and Wanda on that adventure (Willy ended up in jail after beating up Wanda and tearing up their return airplane tickets), we came back home reinvigorated and ready to move mountains.

We even made Mark and Brian a regular part of the show. Anytime either one of us, or a guest on the show, mentioned their names, we immediately pulled out a poster with their pictures on it and began rubbing it reverently while Bill and I chanted, "Come, money, come! Come, money, come!" We thought it was the funniest tribute to a couple of our favorite guys that we could possibly do, and apparently our listeners appreciated it, too.

We put our college interns in pig suits and sent them to promotions for other stations, where they were charged with the task of screaming, at exactly the right time, "The *Rick and Bubba Show* on Q104," loud enough to make it on the competing station's air.

We gave T-shirts to listeners if they could get a shout-out on the air by phone or during a remote broadcast by a competitor. If we did not have a big budget to promote the show, we would just use the competition to help us accomplish it. We did whatever we could to be a nuisance to the other guys, knowing there was no way for them to fight back, no matter how badly we got under their skin. No way but play more songs in a row and read more liner cards.

This was about the time we had to adopt the Guntersville Treaty. A regular part of the show—and our lives away from the show, too, I will admit—were all the practical jokes we played on each other. Because of the competitive nature of Bill, me, Speed Racer (our producer by then), and everyone else on the show, we couldn't allow any prank to go without brutal retaliation. And, of course, the revenge had to be wilder and woollier, more spectacular, more downright dangerous to life and limb than the original stunt. There was an even bigger concern. We were in danger of losing focus if we always had to watch our backs to see if somebody was sawing off the legs of our desk.

This all came to a head with one particular series of practical jokes and subsequent retaliations that took place near the small lakeside town of Guntersville, Alabama. We have been sworn to secrecy about the details of that string of pranks, but I will say it involved an endangered species (a bald eagle), a jealous husband, and a substantial moving cart. It could have resulted in prison time for someone if certain details became known to the authorities. Nobody—and no endangered species—was hurt in this incident, but clearly we had allowed things to go a little bit too far.

Once we realized that the escalating nature of the pranks was actually getting out of hand, that it was distracting us from our bigger goals, we went on the air, in front of our audience and everyone, and announced the drafting and ratification by all involved of the Guntersville Treaty. From that day forward, no practical jokes were permitted among anyone associated with the show, past, present, or future and regardless of the rank or stature of anyone involved. We probably saved many hurt feelings and almost certainly some fractures and stitches by creating and enforcing the treaty. Though there have been some breaches down through the years—with resulting on-air trials and sentencings—we still observe it to this day.

Oh, and it just happens to be some of the funniest live radio many people have ever experienced. Including us!

See, no matter what else we did or what was going on with our careers, we have always continued to have fun on the air. Music became less and less what we did, except for bringing back the disco hit of the day for listeners to identify for a prize. We played the song while Bill told poignant stories about whatever romantic episode in his life the song brought to mind.

When the county-by-county radio ratings came out, nobody could believe it. The two fat boys with the bad hillbilly accents and no promotion budget had beaten the big country music stations, the stations that couldn't be toppled. Even the guys from the major Birmingham stations were impressed that we had taken our zero-dollar promotion budget and fuzzy little signal and had won big-time.

Of course, Bill and I weren't surprised at all. We had simply outworked and outsmarted them. But, in a way, it was sad. They never actually had a chance. Even if they decided to try, nobody could out–Rick-and-Bubba Rick and Bubba.

Still, and though we crowed about it on the air and even stepped up our nuisance campaign, we still needed those other stations to be there, doing the only thing they knew how to do.

We had really won because we were the underdogs, the common men, and we needed to keep letting people know that this was who we were. It wasn't an act.

During that time I won big on another couple of personal fronts, too. My on-air campaign to win the heart of Sherri Bodine had been a lot of fun and an audience favorite. I had written a parody of the Eric Clapton song "Wonderful Tonight," and I interrupted her newscasts to sing it for her. I continued to put listeners on the air, urging them to tell her to give old Rick-Rick a chance. Whether we were on the air or off, her response remained the same. She maintained she only wanted to "be friends." Those, of course, are the unkindest words of all to a guy.

Despite my on-the-air efforts, off the air, I did not push. The truth is, though, that I really was totally infatuated with her. She had a boyfriend for some of that time, but he moved away and they broke up. Only then did she reluctantly agree to go out on a date with me. Then, before it ever happened, she suddenly changed her mind. It was that "just friends" thing again.

Not long after, we were both at the same remote broadcast. Sherri came over to where I was meeting listeners, selling whatever it was we were selling that day. She tried to tell me something, but it was so noisy I couldn't understand what she was saying. Like most disk jockeys and former rock musicians, I have lost a bit of my hearing. I bent down— she's five feet tall and I'm a foot and a half taller—to try to hear what she was telling me.

Then, somehow, we ended up kissing. Not only did I kiss her, but she also kissed me back.

That was it. Neither of us dated anyone again, and she later agreed to become my wife. That turned out to be a much better outcome for an on-air promotion than what eventually happened to that poor possum, Sand Mountain Sam!

Something else was going on, too, and I cannot say for certain that I was aware of it at the time. Most other big-time radio shows, especially in the major markets, were pushing the envelope in their eternal quest for ratings. They were seeing how much they could get away with, how dirty they could be in what they did on the air. They were trying to shock the audience for ratings. Sometimes, unfortunately, that kind of thing will work for a short period of time, and most everything in broadcasting is for short-term success.

Then, inevitably, the smaller markets saw the big-market ratings go up with the filthy programming. Of course, they tried to do the same thing.

Aware of it or not, we were taking our show exactly the opposite way. We didn't do any risqué humor or perform intentionally hurtful stunts. Especially after the ratification of the Guntersville Treaty. Unknowingly, we were just doing what felt right, and in the process, we were bucking the trend. We even alluded sometimes to our faith in Christ, right there on a secular radio show. We caught some grief for it, but neither of us paid much attention to it.

It was us. The show was us. It was working. Case closed.

Things were going well and we had no problem acknowledging whom we really gave credit to. Surprisingly, much of that criticism came not from nonbelievers but from other Christians. It still does. They tell us we should be more somber, more reverential, more ... well, whatever it is that they think good Christians should be.

Maybe they are correct to a point, but we point out that we are entertainers. We want to make people laugh. We have a good time doing it. Bill and I are happy Christians, joyful, and we want to share that joy with everybody who punches us up on the radio dial. We take our faith seriously, but we think we have to be ourselves, too. And ourselves are happy!

Show me the scripture that says we should not laugh and be happy. Go ahead. I'll wait.

See? I didn't think so.

While my life had begun to change a little for the better after teaming up, I wasn't there yet. That had to make it difficult for Bubba.

He had stayed true to his church, to his faith, and he is the kind of Christian who doesn't necessarily preach or push his beliefs on others around him. Instead, he witnesses and demonstrates the power of his religion in the way he lives his life every day and the way he conducts himself in everything he does.

He came with me one night for an appearance in which I did a stand-up routine that was—well—a bit off-color.

"What would have happened if your mother had walked in?" he asked me afterward.

"She would have taken a belt to my behind," I admitted. It did make me think.

Part of it was Sherri. She, too, is a believer who brings others to Christ by example. At that point, before we married, we both had a long way to go. She and I would grow as Christians. That growth would eventually become a big part of the show.

Somewhere about this time, it occurred to me that while we were a couple of wild guys on the radio, and we were having all kinds of fun doing something we loved, there just might be an opportunity for us to do more with what God had given us.

When I was twelve years old, I accepted Christ as my Savior one night after hearing the preacher talk about heaven and hell. The way he put it, heaven seemed the much better choice. If I had to go kneel at the front of the church and eventually get dunked in the baptismal behind the pulpit, then so be it. From that day forward, I was what I call a "cultural Christian." I did my duty and went to church carrying my Bible, but rarely cracked it open any other time. I even became the one who prayed each day on the high school public address system. (Yes, quaint as it sounds, there was a time when prayer was piped throughout the school building!) Truth is, that was another manifestation of show biz. There was Rick, "broadcasting" to all of Oxford High School, reading the prayer each morning while my buddies stifled giggles.

But it would be a while before I began to take my soul's destiny seriously and get my spiritual life in order. Like so many other parts of our lives, it was inevitable that this aspect of ours began to show up on the air during the *Rick and Bubba Show*.

There was nothing false or calculated about it. Religion and faith were important to us. The show was about our lives beyond the radio studio. If we were Christians, then our faith would begin to be a part of the show.

Amazingly, most of our listeners responded positively to it. They sensed that we were as sincere about our spirituality as we were about all the other things we did on the radio. We didn't preach. We didn't force our beliefs on anyone. Nor do we do that now. But during those heady days, as the show evolved, it was beginning to be (and still very much is) an important part of the show.

Then, suddenly, just when things were going so well, the Q was put up for sale and a new owner was on the way.

The new guys had big plans. They were going to pack up and move the transmitter southeast, almost to Birmingham, a much bigger market with many more potential advertising dollars. With the ratings and commercial success we had earned in Gadsden and surrounding areas, and with our recent upturn in the Birmingham ratings book, Bill and I took it for granted that we would be a part of the transition as well, that we would be the Q's morning show after the move. In our minds, we were certain our show would play even better in a bigger market than it did out there in rural Alabama. Mark and Brian's act did just as well in Los Angeles as it had in Birmingham, after all. ("Come, money, come! Come, money, come!")

But speaking of money, our contract was about to come up for renewal, and though we thought we could negotiate from a position of strength, we agreed we wouldn't be looking for a big raise. We figured that the move to the larger market would open up so many more opportunities that we would make it pay off in other ways. We were even beginning to think more about syndication—putting our show on other stations around the country from the new and much bigger base in Birmingham—with the clout of the new owners behind us to help make it happen. With Mark's help, we already had affiliates in Tuscaloosa and

Huntsville, Alabama. We had already been calling ourselves the "Rick and Bubba Network" before we had a single affiliate. It was that old "make it sound big and it will be big" thing again.

We also decided to incorporate the show at that point, and we did. I don't profess to have enough business savvy to have foreseen the value of our incorporating and owning the show rather than just working directly for the station. Even though we were really incorporating nothing, it turned out to be a good move.

Then we were told by the corporate program director for the new company that we most definitely would not go with the Q when it moved. He didn't sugarcoat it, either. He told us the show would never work in a sophisticated market like Birmingham. Instead, they were going to begin searching for a new morning show for the Q. But he told us not to worry. They would try to find us another station in Gadsden, maybe an AM, but otherwise, they made us no promises.

The two "fat boys" were likely done on the Q as soon as our contract was up.

Never mind that Bubba had just built a new house in Jacksonville. He was going to commute to wherever we were until things settled down. Sherri and I had already bought a house in Birmingham. That was partly in anticipation of the move and partly to be close to Brandi and Blake, my kids by my first marriage, who now lived in Birmingham. I was commuting up I-59 every morning.

Oh, and by the way, Sherri and I were about to get some really good news at an especially bad time.

So, was this it? Were we kidding ourselves to think the *Rick and Bubba Show* would forever be anything but small market? Could the corporate program director be right? He did run programming for an exceedingly large broadcasting company, after all. For the first time I began to have doubts about the future of the show. I did some pretty intense praying.

Lord, I thought, *show us a sign, and show it quick!*

10 "We're Test-Driving *You!*"

Unlike my partner, Rick, old Bubba had experience seeing a job go away like a bright sun suddenly covered up by dark clouds. There had been the high hopes and Christian mission of the Jacksonville radio station. Then my making the biggest sale in the TV station's history, seemingly on my way to being a top-tier media sales executive, only to have my accomplishment rewarded by getting handed my walking papers. So I admit that I was worried when we got the news about not making the move to the Birmingham market with the Q.

I prayed about it. I know Rick did, too.

I'm careful not to pray for success or money or glory, or even for our competitors to have bad luck—though it is tempting sometimes. So, instead, I prayed that God would show us the way, help us make the right choices in this thing, and give us strength to get through whatever His plan was for us. And if it was not His will that we take the show to the bigger market, then He would open up another door for us.

Well, maybe I did pray that He would send Betty and me enough thin-sliced bologna and day-old bread to see us through the crisis, if there was to be one. If it was His will.

And it would be extra nice if He could manage just a little bit of Dijon mustard this time . . .

The show was working. I knew it. Rick knew it. Our listeners and sponsors knew it. Shoot, even Arbitron, the people who measure radio listening, knew it. But I guess the word did not make it to the inner sanctum of our new owners' offices.

I can give plenty of examples of what we'd been able to do with all the odds against us. The first time, though, it really sank in that the show had amazing power with listeners was a quick trip we made to one of the textile mills in Fort Payne, Alabama. We'd been getting regular calls from some of the ladies who worked there and listened to the show. Because of the primary product they produced, we had instantly started referring to them on the air as the "sock women." Well, when we got to Fort Payne in the Funmobile, we set up in the parking lot, making sure we could pull away forward, because we still did not have reverse gear in the van at that time. We brought our usual half dozen free T-shirts, fully expecting to have them last for the entire hour we were scheduled to be there.

Not so. We were literally mobbed by the sock women. The shirts were gone instantly, and we were afraid they were going to take the ones off our backs!

Another great example of the traction we were getting actually took place in Birmingham. That was at a time when we were just starting to show up in the ratings down there, even from our little hilltop transmitter in Gadsden and cramped studio behind the skating rink, almost in the Coosa River.

We had conned the Birmingham Barons, the town's Double-A minor league baseball team, into allowing us to play a charity softball game in their ballpark after a Sunday afternoon game. They told us day games on Sundays usually didn't draw much of a crowd, and they didn't think we would have enough people show up to make it worth their while to keep the stadium gates open.

We don't quietly take no for an answer. We believed in this particular cause, and we were convinced we could attract a few hundred paying customers, even way down there in Birmingham on a sultry Sunday afternoon. I guess they figured they might sell an extra snow cone or two, or maybe they just got tired of getting calls from us, but the Barons' management finally reluctantly agreed.

That Sunday, as the team representatives predicted, the stands were essentially empty for the Barons game. But then, as the last few innings wound down, an odd thing started happening. The crowd grew. From the press box, people could see cars lined up, coming toward the stadium.

As our little ragtag team started stretching and warming up, we looked up to see the stands almost full. About thirteen thousand people were there that day for a Rick and Bubba charity softball game!

With that success fresh in our memories, the time came to turn on the transmitter from the new location, to blanket the Birmingham market with the Q, and with Rick and Bubba still doing the morning show for at least a few weeks longer. At this point we still hadn't been told for certain that we were out, but neither was anyone in much of a hurry to renew our contract. It was clear, too, that no money was going to be spent on promotion or advertising for the station until the issue of the new morning show was settled.

So Rick, who had been driving up from Birmingham every morning to do the show, enjoyed the much shorter commute after the studios went live in the new market. I just stayed in our new house not far from my mother in Jacksonville, wondering if Betty and I should sell, stay, or go buy a trailer, pull it behind the truck, and live out of that thing until everything settled down.

Then the new owners sent their main programming guy down to visit with us. He wanted to go up the mountain to see the new transmitter plant, and since I was still the chief engineer (that job was threatening to go away, too, by the way), I agreed to take him. He, Rick, and the Birmingham market manager all went along. It was on that trip that the program exec shared our fates with us. To his credit, he pulled no punches.

"You know, I came down here to test-drive you guys, listen to the show, see what we might be able to do to tweak it and make it work. We've decided that we don't think your type of show will work in Birmingham. It's not the way we are going to take the station," he told us.

We were stunned. Oh, we wouldn't have been surprised to hear that they might want to cut our pay or do something else to try to run us off. Or even that they wanted to go in another direction. But for some odd reason, we didn't expect to be insulted.

Then he tried to flatter us, in a very backhanded way.

"See, fellows, your ratings are pretty good up here in this small market. But you are too good for the rest of the station. You're sucking the life out of it."

Well, I had to admit that was a novel way of looking at it. Go for a mediocre morning show so the rest of the station can stay consistently mediocre. That is some high-level broadcast strategy there!

I couldn't hold my tongue any longer. I told him exactly what I thought.

"Well, I don't think you quite understand," I blurted out. "You are not test-driving us. We're test-driving *you!*"

I don't know where that prideful outburst came from. It was totally out of character for me, it was not the way I was raised, but I was mad. It felt like he'd been insulting us since the moment we met.

It didn't matter. My statement didn't even seem to faze the fellow. He told us he would appreciate it if we honored our contract and maybe even stayed on a little after it expired if need be, working with the station now that it was in Birmingham. Then, when they had a new morning show in place on the Q, they might be able—*might* be able, understand—to put us on a station in Gadsden. Maybe.

There was also a strong hint that if we did anything dramatic on the air, such as even insinuate that we might be getting the shaft, it could be considered a breach of our weak little contract. Then we would not even be blessed with a slot on an AM station, one so high up the dial the *Rick and Bubba Show* would emanate from the glove box.

117

Instead, we would be out of a job. And what other savvy broadcaster would be crazy enough to hire a couple of fat guys with hillbilly accents who refused to play "the hits"?

"God is testing us," I kept telling myself, Rick, Betty, and anybody else who would listen. "God is testing us, and He has a plan for us."

But would it be asking too much for Him to give us a tiny hint or two about what that plan might be?

11 "...Think of Us!"

Job. No job. Job. No job.

I—Rick—will admit I was scared. I had never been out of a job since I got that first one with my dad's help in Anniston. Sherri and I had just bought a house. Though I had eventually graduated from Jacksonville State University with my very beneficial sociology degree, I had no idea how to make a living doing anything besides being silly on the radio.

But you know what? By this point in my life, I was putting things in God's hands, trusting He would help find a way.

Of course, that didn't stop us from playing a little hardball!

So there we were, doing the show on the Q with Birmingham listeners now able to hear us loud and clear. We knew that the ratings numbers we had already seen would only go up, but we had no reason to hope that we would be around to enjoy the benefits when those ratings came out after the holidays. We were in serious limbo, not knowing if each day's *Rick and Bubba Show* would be our last or not. When we said good-bye to our great listeners on Fridays, we had no way of knowing if we would be back on Monday morning or not.

On the air, Bubba and I didn't do anything different. We had fun with listeners and anybody we could convince to stop by the studio, including a long list of celebrities, comedians, station employees, authors hawking books, and a wonderful assortment of oddball but

Bubba shows everyone why he is clearly one of the sexiest fat men alive. Charity Pro AM

real characters who somehow gravitated to us and our un-radio style of radio. We talked about simple adventures, like funny things that happened while going to the supermarket, family trips to Six Flags, my kids' ball games, what happened at the drive-through at Burger Doodle last night. We were working church in there, too, and some of the funny stories came from Sunday school class or our preacher friends. We kept up the assault on the other stations as well, but our pranks and jabs were now aimed at a whole different bunch of them. Bigger markets or not, they still made easy targets.

We were doing a remote broadcast from a big charity Seniors Tour golf tournament one morning. As was typical, we were having fun causing chaos all around us, interviewing a long list of celebrities who all seemed to be having as much fun as we were when they visited our little folding table, even if they sometimes didn't quite know how to take us and our kind of off-the-wall radio show.

We were having a blast shooting foam rockets at the other radio and TV stations set up and broadcasting—from much more elaborate remote setups—just down the way from us. It was especially fun disrupting them while they were interviewing those same celebrities who had just been on the air with us. We also had interns and listeners doing all they could to get "Rick and Bubba" blurted out on their air.

During the broadcast Andy Spinosi just happened to stop by for a visit. He was a member of the morning show cast at classic rock powerhouse Rock 99. At first we thought he'd come over to retaliate for all the foam rockets we'd been shooting in their direction all morning, but he just wanted to hang out. Without even thinking about it or requesting permission from the home office, we put him on the air and had a ball talking and riffing with him. He was a naturally funny individual, a friend of the show even if he did work for the competition, and we all three played off each other as if we had been doing a three-man show for years.

Andy could not believe we put him—an important member of a competing station's morning show—on the air for everyone to hear. In those days—and it's still pretty much the case—there is a sacrosanct rule that you don't even mention, let alone acknowledge the existence of, another radio station on your own air. We sort of figure listeners are smart enough to know that other stations exist and people have the option of simply hitting a button anytime they want to and giving them a listen, whether we mention them on the air or not.

Andy became a great friend of the show and later did funny things with us when we worked for the same company. Unfortunately, he passed away a few years ago, and we still miss him.

Since the owners were not yet spending a penny to promote the new station's move to the Birmingham market while they sought that elusive new morning show to replace us, we had to rely on our typical and well-proven guerrilla marketing tactics to promote the show. That was nothing new, and we were well aware of what it took to get it done.

But now we had to turn it up a notch. Anyplace two or more people gathered, we were there in our latest low-rent version of the Funmobile. We printed up and sold T-shirts with a caricature of Bubba and me. We also offered baby bibs, baseball caps, hunting camo, and anything else we could think of that the manufacturer would let us have on consignment. We continued to award prizes for anyone who could get a "Rick and Bubba" sign on one of the local TV shows or managed to give us a shout-out on another radio station. It seemed as if those stations worried more about one of our folks getting in a plug for us than they did about what else was going out on the air. We reserved special prizes for those listeners who managed to get something with our names or logo on national media, and a bunch of them were able to do it.

As usual, our listeners happily did their part. Let me say again how wonderful those early adopters of the show were. It couldn't have been easy to admit they listened to us hillbillies from Gadsden, reading Shakespeare with a drawl and doing telethons for possums. Yet they embraced us, did what we asked of them, and helped make us look good at promotions, charity softball games, remote broadcasts, sponsor locations, and much more. The only way we could ever pay them back is to make them laugh. That and stay true to who we are.

We told them that when they saw a competing radio station's billboard: "Think of us. Their billboards are our billboards! No matter whose call letters are on it, that's a 'Rick and Bubba' billboard." Or if they saw another radio station's commercial on television, just think about Rick and Bubba. They did! And they talked about it and told their friends about it.

As those who listen to the show know, I spend a lot of time hanging out at various ball fields, what with all my kids and their interest in sports. It was shortly after we made the rather tenuous move to Birmingham that I had two key encounters at ball fields.

One of those rattled me severely. The other one was simply God putting me and another party together in the right place at the right time.

I was in the bleachers, watching one of my daughter Brandi's softball games one afternoon, spending about as much time carrying on a running commentary with the other parents as I did watching her play. Sherri had been feeling poorly the previous few days and had a doctor's appointment, so she was running late for the game.

Then I saw Sherri coming my way from across the parking lot. My first thought was, *Rick Burgess, you are the luckiest son of a gun on the planet for having that woman as your wife.*

Then a feeling hit me that I cannot even begin to describe. It was a mixture of elation and cold, cold fear.

Sherri came up the bleachers and sat next to me. She gave me a quick kiss. I knew that look on her face, the smile. She was excited about something, and she was bursting to tell me what it was, but she was not sure how.

"Well, honey, I have something to tell you," she started, and her eyes were immediately shining with tears. "I wanted to wait until we got home, but . . ."

"You are pregnant," I told her matter-of-factly.

She looked at me, wide-eyed.

"How did you know?"

I hugged her, kissed her, even as the oddest mix of emotions continued to flood through me. I knew how much she wanted children, how pleased she was to be pregnant with our first child.

She had more than a little idea of the predicament the show was in, how shaky our future was at the moment, but I think she had supreme confidence that things would work out for the best. *Supreme* being the operative word. She had confidence in me, but she also knew God would take care of us. That's a wonderful confidence to have at a time like that!

As the thought of being an out-of-work-bum of a dad entered my brain, I admit I was not as totally convinced as she was that everything would be okay. But I knew all I could do was the best I could do.

Still, the holidays were quickly approaching, Bill and I had two-week vacations coming up that would have us out of pocket for the rest of the year, and we had no idea if we would have jobs or not when we got back.

Merry Christmas and Happy New Year to you, too!

Bill and Betty had a trip planned to Chicago, and they decided to go ahead and enjoy the sights of the Windy City. Bill had no idea where he was supposed to go back to when they got back home. Our contracts expired at the end of the year, during our vacation.

Did our new bosses want us to show up and go back on the air on the Q, just as if everything was hunky-dory? Or did we need to start checking with the peanut-whistle AM stations in Gadsden to see if we were supposed to be on the air up there somewhere?

Well, we just went on back to the Q after the New Year and kept doing our thing, knowing that the other shoe was likely to drop any minute. Neither of us would have been surprised if the program director came in and pulled us off the air in the middle of a show.

Still, we were having more fun than ever once the "On Air" light flashed on every day at 6:00 a.m. I would still bet that our listeners had no idea at the time about the turmoil Bill and I were going through in our personal and professional lives. I am proud to say that we kept all that out of the studio, off the air, away from all the fun we were having with our new bunch of regular listeners.

We were breaking our number one rule. We were not bringing our lives to the show. We had no choice, though.

Then I was at my oldest son, Blake's, football game one day, talking with one of the other parents. Somewhere in the conversation, the fellow I was talking with casually mentioned that he was a trial lawyer and had done a case or two that involved radio stations. He introduced himself as David Marsh. I gave him a thumbnail sketch of our situation with our contract, and he told me to give him a call if we needed any help. I took his card, shoved it into my wallet, and promptly forgot about it.

I didn't know at the time that David was one of the top attorneys in the state. God's hand putting us at the same ball game at the same time? I think so. No, I know so.

Then, with everything still in limbo, the Arbitron book came out. That's a big deal in the radio station business. The ratings are what stations live and die by. Not only does it estimate how many listeners each station has, but it also allows those who do well to charge much more money for commercials. Ratings are the lifeblood of a station.

The station program director—who was doing all he could to hurry up and show us the door—came into the studio, wide-eyed, a printout of the ratings in his hand. The Q, with no promotion and those two hillbillies from Gadsden making a travesty of the station's morning show, was number two in Birmingham! Number two, surpassed only slightly by the legendary country music station WZZK.

To be honest, Bubba and I were a little disappointed that we were not number one. I think it was Richard Petty who said that coming in second in any race meant that you were just the first loser. But being a close number two to a station that had been number one for a decade only proved that the magic was still working.

God was still blessing the *Rick and Bubba Show*.

Suddenly everyone's attitude about the show and its two overweight hosts seemed to change. We didn't try to hide the fact that Bill and I were getting feelers from other stations, from in and out of town, wondering what our deal was with the Q. Word was out that we were working without a contract, that we might be available.

The next day the program director walked into the studio while Bubba and I were still on the air. For those who have visited us, you know what a loud, chaotic scene it is during our little radio program. He stood there and waited for us to hoot and yell and carry on about something before we finally went to commercials.

"Guys, we wanted to let you know that we would like to revisit your contract and keep you on the air here at the Q." He smiled, looking ever so much like a cow eating saw briars. I can only imagine how much it hurt him to admit that he and his corporate program director had been wrong.

Bill and I looked at each other. Our first inclination was to say, "Yes! Where do we sign?"

I had two kids and a baby on the way, plus a healthy new mortgage. Bubba had house payments, and he and Betty wanted to start a family, too. By the way, we both really, really enjoyed eating.

We needed jobs.

Truth is, we were already making more money than we ever dreamed we would make in radio. I already talked about my dad leaving his coaching job and moving his family to Oxford to be head football coach and athletic director for the princely sum of fourteen thousand a year. I think either one of us would have been happy to just sign on for the same salary we were making in exchange for a little security.

Then the program director took a sheet of paper from his coat pocket and shoved it over to a spot on the control board, about half-way between where Bubba and I sat facing each other. It lay there between our microphones for a moment. We were both afraid to pick it up and read it.

"Just sign this so you can feel better about the whole thing and we can work out the details and get you a formal contract sometime in the next few days," he told us. Then he left the studio.

As the last of the commercials in the spot break played out, Bill and I hastily read the one short sentence on the paper that he had put in front of us.

"By our signature below, we agree to sign a renewal contract when it is presented to us."

I stifled a laugh. The look on Bill's face was priceless.

They were asking us to agree to terms of a contract we had never even seen! That was almost as insulting as the things the corporate program director had told us that day at the new transmitter site.

After the show was over, we went to the station manager's office. He urged us to sign the paper so we could be assured of staying on the Q. Somewhere during the conversation I stepped out of the office and fished a business card out of my wallet. I used my cell phone and dialed the number on the card.

"Could I speak to David Marsh, please?"

The attorney was on the line shortly. We told him what had just happened.

"Don't talk to anybody," he told me. "Get out of there right now. Come straight to see me."

I got Bubba, and we tried to leave the office, as David advised. You ever see two fat guys trying to be stealthy? Hiding behind potted plants and lobby furniture while we worked our way to the elevator, all without talking to anybody? It was a sight to see, I am sure, but we got away and hurried directly to David's office.

You don't have to be Perry Mason to figure out what he advised us to do. He wanted us to allow him to speak with other radio stations and let them know we were now officially free agents. And, of course, he advised us not to sign anything, no matter how badly we needed jobs.

The next day, when we told our program director we would not be signing his agreement-to-agree-to-who-knows-what and that David Marsh was now representing us in the negotiations, he turned white in the face and left the room. We later learned that David had represented a former employee of the station in an employment dispute. They were quite familiar with Bubba's and my brand-new lawyer.

So there came a fateful day with Bill and me sitting there in David's office while he did what he does so well. He was on the telephone with one station group after another, listening, talking, scratching out notes on a legal pad to let us know what was happening on the other end of the line.

This was all new to us. Again, we were all set to start sending out tapes and résumés, looking for a job anywhere they had a transmitter on the air, just to keep the show on the radio and a paycheck coming in. Also, we had already decided that if the Q wanted us to stay, we would sign with them, basically agreeing to the same one-sided contract for the same amount of money as before, just to keep the show going. And a nice paycheck coming in. And medical insurance. That was the kind of thing that might come in handy with a baby on the way.

Now, here we were, in the office of a high-powered attorney, listening to him negotiate. If it hadn't been our futures being bandied about, it would have been quite entertaining watching David work, swinging

129

away at the best pitches from some managers and owners of radio stations. We knew them by name and reputation to be very good fastball pitchers. There he was, throwing out and scratching numbers on the pad that took our breath away.

It was nerve-racking. Bill spent much of that day in a fetal position on David's couch. I looked as if I were being jolted by periodic shocks of electricity. As usual, I could not be still and jumped up and paced around the office, trying to work off all that nervous energy before I exploded in a puff of smoke.

At one point Bill actually got physically sick from the tension and had to go to the men's room. When he came back, the number on the pad had doubled from what it was when he left the room. I thought he was going to have to leave again when he realized what had happened.

"Okay, then," Marsh finally told somebody on the other end of the telephone. "Sounds like we have an agreement in principle. Let me discuss your offer with my clients and I'll get back to you shortly."

We couldn't believe it. We had stepped into David Marsh's office that day, little more than a sad pair of unemployed disk jockeys. Now we had an offer in front of us—after a serious bidding war with representatives of some of the largest radio group owners in the world—that was more than three times what we were making before. It included a commitment to promote the show, to build us a studio all our own, and to allow us to pay a decent wage to a few key members of the team who contributed so much to our success, and more.

I am not a greedy person, but it is good to feel wanted. If that "want" is measured in U.S. currency, then all the better. More than anything, though, having people throwing around the kind of numbers we had seen scrawled on David's scratch pad validated what Bill and I were trying to do with the show—to be real and respect the listeners as we brought our own families, friends, and faith to the show. We were trying to do a good job for the sponsors who support us. And we were having a whale of a lot of fun doing it.

There was one other thing, though. The company that wanted us the most—and the ones who were willing to write the largest check—was Dick Broadcasting, an independent station owner, and not one of the big conglomerates.

And the station they wanted to put us on?

94.5 WYSF. The former WAPI-FM. I-95. The same station where Mark and Brian had first started their show years before.

Come, money, come! Come, money, come!

12   Van Man, Errand Boy, and the Crazy Sign Man

We've been fortunate to be associated with a number of people who played a big role in the success of the *Rick and Bubba Show*. We've mentioned some of them already, including our wives, families, and spiritual mentors. Of course, we couldn't have done it without the folks who listened, called in, showed up, told other people about us, wore our shirts and ball caps, risked life and limb to hold up signs or yell out our names on other media, and understood what we were trying to do.

There has been a whole flock of others who played big roles, too. People who got up early, worked hard, did embarrassing things on our behalf, and took a chance of getting pummeled for the show, usually for fun and fame but always for very little—and sometimes not any—pay.

But they helped Rick and me become Rick and Bubba. Helped mightily, and I hope they know how much we appreciate every single one of them.

***

Rick knew a hyper young man named Calvin Wilburn from their days in radio at the same time in Anniston. Then later, when Q104 was in need of a part-time announcer, Rick gave him a call. As so often happened with most everything we have done in the exciting world of radio broadcasting, we kind of abducted Calvin from his real job and accidentally made him a key part of the *Rick and Bubba Show*.

We needed somebody to go out and do wild and crazy things on our behalf, and he was willing and able. That and he did such a darn good job of it. He became our "guy on location." He did all those stunts so successfully and was so funny in the process while remaining unbelievably fearless that we often sent him off to do things we probably should have reconsidered. (Fearless, though you could not tell it during some of those adventures.) Some of our interns and he visited haunted houses around Halloween each year. Even Calvin would admit that you could hear the fear in his voice when we played back those hilarious recordings.

Rick and I were in agreement from the beginning, though, that once Calvin was a regular part of the show, he had to have another name. "Calvin Wilburn" sounded like a radio evangelist's name, or the brand name of some Kentucky sippin' whiskey. That would never do.

Since he spent so much time running around in the various incarnations of our Fun-mobile van, we started calling him "Van Man." Someone suggested that he sort of favored the cartoon character Johnny Quest, so we used that for a while, too.

Finally, because of the way he was constantly in motion, zooming from adventure to adventure in that old smoking van, getting into deep trouble and then out of it by the end of the show each day, we came up with another cartoon character that fit better: Speed Racer.

The name stuck, though we've long since shortened it to "Speedy."

Regular listeners know how much Speedy has meant to the show and how hard he's worked to make it what it has become. He graduated from running errands, tracking down free food, and riding herd on overeager fans to actually producing the show. That job pretty much means doing all the stuff that Rick and I don't want to do because we have to go eat lunch or take a nap.

In addition to all the stuff he has been doing for the show from the beginning—including making sure we always have plenty of free food—he books guests, tracks down material for our various segments, keeps us on track and on time, and puts the stopwatch on the celebrities, sports mascots, and just regular people who stop by to run the 40-yard dash outside our studio window. He also oversees the interns, referees pickup basketball games and lawn mower races, keeps track of the show archives for the Internet site and "best of" CDs, runs the show when Rick and I are on vacation or traveling promoting books and lobbying for the Pulitzer Prize, and much more.

And did I mention Speedy's most important job—making sure we have plenty of free food? Doing a morning radio show makes a man really hungry, and we owe it to our listeners to not allow ourselves to grow weak.

Speedy, too, married very well since he joined the show. He and his family have literally become part of and grown up on the show, just as Rick's and mine have. That, too, has provided plenty of real and embarrassingly personal material we are perfectly willing to share with millions of listeners every morning.

I can't remember exactly how we began incorporating interns into the show. It's almost a joke in the broadcasting business that stations take young, eager college students who dream of media careers, who want to learn the ropes and get an inside, realistic look at the business, and then they promptly put them to work counting T-shirts, washing the station van, and doing menial labor for no salary. Rick and I decided early on that we'd make our interns an integral part of the show. We would not only pull back the curtain and allow them to see what really went on during a radio show. We would also make their love lives, triumphs and failures, personal foibles, and true-life experiences as public as ours were. This came in the spirit of giving them real-world experience in the business of radio.

Of course, it also provides free entertainment for our vast listening audience. When all else fails, we can get one of those kids on the microphone and talk about the intimate details of the previous weekend's date or about how things are going in school. Despite this, we've had hundreds of people willing to sign on as Rick and Bubba interns.

Our very first intern was a kid named Louie. He didn't last long. His mother believed Rick and I were bad influences on him and made him quit. We still can't imagine why she thought that about us.

But our second intern was perfect for the job. He had no discernible skills other than going and getting stuff, so Rick immediately named him "Errand Boy," and that started the long-standing tradition of giving our interns nicknames. It was fun to discuss name possibilities on the air and come up with the very one that perfectly summed up his or her personality. We usually still allow the audience to suggest names, typically based on an intern's appearance, interests, or mannerisms. Can it be embarrassing for them? Sure! But, like everything else we put our interns through, it's also entertaining.

There is a practical and serious reason for using intern nicknames on the air, though. We are aware that these are usually kids, college students, and if we use their real names on the air, they may be subject to harassment from the lunatic fringe out there. Better that we allow them to be as anonymous as we can, even as we embarrass the fool out of them.

Errand Boy eventually left—we understand he's in law enforcement somewhere, which is unsettling to think about—and we brought on our third intern. He was a tall, skinny, athletic kid whom we promptly dubbed "Don Juan DeMarco" Williams, or just "Don Juan" or "Dee." Of course, we had many other names for him, including "Creamy Smooth Brother," since he was—and I assume still is—African-American.

We had a lot of fun with Don Juan, when we started the Rick and Bubba basketball team to play charity games around the area. Charity or not—regardless of the game—Rick and I are fiercely competitive. We play first to win, then to make money for the cause. We are perfectly willing to bring on ringers, such as former Major League Baseball

All-Star Todd Jones, to make sure we accomplish our first goal: beating the whey out of whoever we play.

We were sure Don Juan would be our basketball team ringer since he was tall and athletic. But when we saw him with a basketball for the first time, our hopes were dashed. He looked like a radio tower falling down. Basketball was not Dee's talent!

Thankfully Don Juan was a very capable young man in other key areas and quickly moved from intern to full-time staff member. He was blessed with an infectious laugh, a great outlook on life, and the hilarious inability to say the word *Buick*. Naturally, we called upon him to say "Buick" on the show every chance we got.

Our merchandise business had grown tremendously, so we put him in charge of managing that aspect of the show, along with many other mostly thankless jobs. Jobs like going to get us food. Of course, he still played a big part on the air, too.

As the staff grew, we began referring to ourselves during the show by numbers. Rick was "Number One," I was "Number Two," Speedy was "Number Three," and Don Juan became "Number Four."

He was also musically talented and wrote and produced many songs and a lot of the bumper music for the show. Don Juan eventually left us to go to Virginia to study record producing and recording.

In addition to the long list of interns, we've also been fortunate enough to have regular characters—unpaid characters, by the way—who have contributed to our success and to what the *Rick and Bubba Show* has become.

For example, we answered the telephone one day and the person on the other end was pretending—in a very funny way—to be a typical radio newsman, complete with over-the-top voice and a tendency to say "Good morning!" a lot. "Roger Lewis" became a regular *Rick and Bubba Show* correspondent, delivering hilarious news reports on whatever the big topic of the day happened to be. What made it so funny was that he seemed to really be doing his best to be serious. It tied in very well with a running bit we did since the early days in Gadsden, making life miserable for somber newsmen like the great Dave Fitz.

"Roger" was actually a producer for a show on WABC Radio in New York City whom we met during one of our junkets to the big city. He loved what we were doing and was only too glad to join the fun.

We've always had groups of people who just show up outside of whatever studio we happen to be broadcasting from at the time. They're there hoping to give a shout-out to friends or family if any of us go outside with a microphone. They also hope to participate in some of the stunts we so often do, usually on the spur of the moment, and we don't mind at all. We appreciate the loyalty of these folks who are willing to come and stand in rain and sleet and baking sun and wave to us. We even took that into consideration when we moved to our latest digs, picking a place with big windows, as much so we could see the crowd and feed off their energy as to allow them to see us. It is an area that is covered, out of the elements, and we included a small seating area in our studio—the "golden ticket" seats—so we could allow folks to come in and be a part of the show.

Some of the people who have shown up outside of our studios through the years have scared us. One such regular visitor was not having much luck attracting our attention, so he began making big signs with slogans and sayings written on them. He held them up so we could see them from our window on the fourth floor. Heck! People could've seen them from the Space Shuttle! Of course, we had no choice. We acknowledged him and his crazy signs on the air.

It was also inevitable that we give him a name. When we found out that his first name was Jim, the rest was obvious. He became "Jim, the Crazy Sign Man."

What else could you name somebody who stood out in all kinds of weather just to wave signs at two goobers on the radio? Actually, except when he was painting and holding up signs for the radio audience, Jim is a very intelligent and well-read individual, an employee of the local public library system. Other than his odd sign-waving habit, he is a perfectly normal human being. Amazingly, Jim is a world-class Scrabble player and successfully participates in competitions all over the planet.

So, in light of that, I take back what I said about him being a perfectly normal and sane human being.

There was also a kid who first started calling in to the show when we did a thing we called "Pigskin Roundup" on football Friday nights back in Gadsden. That was supposed to be a high school football scoreboard show, but it really became a parody of all those small-market shows we had heard growing up. That and an excuse to have people bring us food from area stadium concession stands for evaluation so we could name the "Rick and Bubba High School Concession Stand of the Week."

This kid made up hilarious songs and played them for us over the telephone, accompanied by a small electronic keyboard. He later showed up—uninvited, of course—and began hanging around the radio station. As have so many others who craved a career in radio, he refused to leave until the program director gave him a part-time weekend deejay job. Sort of like us, he really didn't have a radio voice, and he didn't fit the rigid read-the-cards-and-shut-up style that stations wanted then. Or now, for that matter. He was, though, a naturally funny and very creative guy.

You guessed it. We started allowing him to hang out with us during the show, even though we never knew what was going to come out of his mouth or what sort of handle he would get himself into when he was away from the station. Regardless, he was more than willing to share those experiences with our listeners and us. They were always funny, if not horrifying.

He was also willing to go out and do dumb and potentially illegal things with Speedy and Don Juan. He had to have a name, so Rick came up with the perfect one, based on his brand of electronic keyboard. He became "Casio Kid."

Casio also sported a total lack of responsibility. If he was supposed to be somewhere at 7:00 a.m., we told him he had to show up at 6:00 a.m. That way, he might get there by 7:30. His excuses for never being on time were always hilarious.

We had a lot of fun with Casio when he eventually became a sales assistant for the station after we moved to 94.5 WYSF in Birmingham. He was the least likely "sales type" you would ever want to meet. We couldn't imagine him making an appointment and showing up for it, or somehow helping close a deal, getting a contract signed, and actually making it back to the station with it. Of course, even though he was supposed to be out doing buttoned-up, professional things, helping the sales staff pitch business, he still spent lots of time in the studio with us. Or was out doing very unprofessional stunts on behalf of the show. Or he was in the production studio for hours with Don Juan, putting together rap songs and parodies for the show.

We couldn't believe it when Casio marched in one day and told us he was leaving Birmingham, moving to Los Angeles, and starting a career as a stand-up comic. Many of you probably heard the kidding we gave him for that brilliant career move. And you probably also remember our shock the day he called in and told us he was going to be a regular on the *Tonight Show with Jay Leno*. Maybe it was more disbelief than shock, but nonetheless, we hooted over that news, too.

Until it turned out to be true, that is. Casio actually did do a series of bits on the Leno show, very similar to what he had once done for no compensation whatsoever on the *Rick and Bubba Show*. Casio is now enjoying a successful career as a stand-up comic, under the name Matt Mitchell, and still stops in to the show on occasion. Never at the time he promises, of course. Or we have no idea he is coming until he shows up. We still wonder if the comedy club owners tell him his set will begin at 7:00 p.m. so he will be there by 8:30 for an 8:00 gig.

Speaking of stereotypes, we had another accidental regular on the show who provided many special moments, a young man of Middle Eastern descent who—yes, it's true—ran a convenience store. He had an unpronounceable name, so we called him "Killy Vanilly." Killy called in regularly, talking about his adventures getting acclimated to his new life in America. Rick gave him a really rough time on the air, but Killy kept coming back for more. Finally, when he told us he was going to Atlanta to take the test necessary to become a naturalized American citizen, we knew we had to help him as only the *Rick and Bubba Show* could do.

We assigned Speedy the job of making sure Killy got to the federal building where the test was to be given. They left early in the morning, driving the latest version of the Funmobile, to be sure they got there in time. They checked in regularly during the show that morning, keeping the audience updated. We all—including the Rick and Bubba Army, our listeners—had taken a real interest in Killy and his quest to become a citizen.

Well, as usual, that adventure turned out to be a classic. The highlight for me was probably Speedy using a bullhorn to scream out facts about American history from the top of the parking deck adjacent to the immigration office building in downtown Atlanta. Killy was inside, presumably taking the naturalization test, and Speedy did not want him to forget how many original colonies there were or who the fifth president of the United States was.

I don't know if that loud form of a cheat sheet was what did the trick or not, but Killy did pass the exam, become a naturalized citizen, and eventually left his job at the convenience store. We still hear from him sometimes, and he is doing well.

Another favorite on the show was School Closing Tony. Tony was a young man who had suffered a debilitating brain injury but fought with all his might to live as normal a life as he could. Not only was he an inspiration to us, but he was also a very funny addition, usually unintentionally. After he said something that really tickled us, he would quip in his endearing, self-deprecating way, "I just ain't right!" He got his nickname because he first began calling in to the show—totally on a volunteer basis—to let us know which schools, businesses, and highways would be closed that morning due to a rare Alabama snowfall.

Real and funny. The people who have contributed to the show down through the years have certainly fit that description.

So do all the real-life experiences Rick and I and the folks on the show bring to the air every time we turn on a microphone. That's true, even when the events we discuss are potentially tragic.

A good example is the time Betty and I were almost murdered at church. We were at services one day at Jacksonville Baptist Church, sitting in the back pew the way all Baptists are required to do, when our pastor told us we were going to have an emergency drill right after the preaching. That happened regularly. We live in a highly tornado-prone area, so we held such practice evacuations often, working on leaving the church and getting to a safer structure if there should be a warning issued. I didn't enjoy them because they inevitably happened on hot days and, like most fat folks, I sweat a bunch. It also postponed dismissal after the end of the sermon, which unfortunately delayed the highlight of my week: Sunday dinner. Still, I understood the need, even if I was staining the armpits of my dress shirt and my stomach sounded like the distant rumble of thunder.

One morning when we were in the parking lot, awaiting the word to go back inside, we suddenly heard something that sounded like the crack of a whip.

"That sounded like a gunshot," Betty said. I've never asked her how she knew what a gunshot sounded like. That was well before Rick and I had gotten so deep into hunting, but I knew what a gunshot sounded like. It did actually sound like a small-caliber weapon of some kind, but I figured firecrackers, maybe.

Then, from the far edge of the crowd, we saw a woman running in a panic, her arms in the air. Right behind her was a guy with a rifle, waving it around, shooting at the woman.

Well, that was a novel twist to our usual worship service! Usually about the most exciting thing that happened was when Brother McGuire napped during the message and talked in his sleep.

As we stood there, staring in disbelief, the gunman turned toward a clump of us Baptists and pulled the trigger. The bullet whizzed over our heads.

I did the only thing I knew to do. I grabbed Betty and hit the ground. There were only two thoughts on my mind at that point. One was to get Betty and my mother—who was at church with us, as usual—inside and to a safe place. The other was, *Wow! This will be all over the network and cable newscasts soon, and that has to be good for the show!*

Well, we did manage to get inside without getting ourselves shot. We made it to a women's restroom and spent several stifling minutes in there with family, friends, and fellow perspiring Baptists. And School Closing Tony. He was in there with us, too.

Thankfully, the police arrived and arrested the man with the rifle. I guess all those accumulated prayers worked, because nobody was hurt.

Now, I mention this to make the point about how every little adventure any of us experiences is fair game to end up as a segment on the show. For those who heard it, you know how funny it was to retell this one the next day. Real events. Real funny. Even when it wasn't so comical while we were lying there in the church parking lot, sweating, trembling, stomachs growling, with bullets flying over our heads.

I will also mention that there would come a time when some actual, real-life occurrences became a key part of the show, even though they were not funny either. Real. Not always funny.

That's one of the things we think has led to the success of the *Rick and Bubba Show*. People know that we are being ourselves. The events we recount and the people who become part of the show—from interns to regulars—are, too.

I hope those people who did contribute so much know how deeply we appreciate it, even if we don't mention them all here. And those who say we shouldn't bring our real lives, our families, our everyday experiences to the show realize that we couldn't have done it any differently, even if we'd tried.

13 God Is Great

When I speak to church groups, people often ask, "Rick, why does God let bad things happen, even when we pray for something better?" It is the age-old question. One that pops up in the Bible often.

Why does God let bad things happen to people? Why do believers still have bad things happen to them? Why do even the strongest believers hurt? Why do innocent children suffer?

I have the answers to these questions. Or at least, I know where to find those answers. One place is 1 Peter, chapter 1. There are plenty more.

I do believe that we need to have enough faith to get us through those times. When we are tested, that is when we have to be strongest in our faith.

One thing I know: we have no way to anticipate when those tests are coming. Just that when everything is rocking along and we are on top of the world, we'd best be bracing ourselves.

In fact, the better things are going, the bigger the trial we'd best be getting ready to endure.

———

After making the move from the Q, Bubba and I quickly settled into our new digs at Dick Broadcasting (unfortunate name but a great place to work). Thank goodness, our loyal listeners followed us right down the FM dial from 103.7 to 94.5. We simply picked up right where we left off, doing the same kind of reality-based conversation and goofy stunts that had gotten us to near the top of the ratings. We continued to poke fun at the other radio stations, too, knowing they couldn't and wouldn't poke back.

Since most of them still didn't understand what we were doing—even though they had tried to hire us to come over to their place to do it—and since they were still locked into the accepted formula for formatted, consultant-driven radio, we knew we continued to have them right where we wanted them. They would never even think about doing what it would take to beat us; not so long as we listened to our audience and continued to work and work and work and never got lazy. While we were strong in our convictions about what would work on the radio, I'm not so sure our new employers were totally convinced yet. The general manager of the station was a Birmingham radio veteran named Davis Hawkins. It was Davis who had convinced

Dick Broadcasting to spend so much money luring a couple of loud fat boys over to 94.5 WYSF. More money than anyone had ever been paid in the market before.

It was a huge gamble. We were about as un-radio as anyone could be. Sure, we had the one big rating book at the Q, but many in the industry were convinced it was only the novelty of our show that created that spike in the numbers. Our act would soon wear thin, and "more music in the mornings" would be resurgent. No doubt Davis had his moments of heartburn as he listened to what he had put on WYSF for four hours every weekday morning during drive time. He'd wagered his career on us.

It was about this time that we accomplished one of our most audacious feats. Bill and I came up with the idea for a live event, a concert featuring only the people from the radio show and a few of our friends. There would be no stars or anybody who would be a big audience draw. Just our buddies and us playing music and having a good time and maybe selling a T-shirt or two. In a way, it would be like those shows my brother, Greg, and the kids in Cheaha Acres used to put on back in our carport in Oxford.

The name was obvious: "Fat Fest."

Somehow we convinced the operators of the big outdoor concert venue south of Birmingham to host the show for very little money. I figure they were counting on selling a few hot dogs and breaking even and would benefit from all the mentions we'd give them on the air.

The lineup included—besides Bubba and me—some of the regular members of the show staff, as well as comedian Mickey Dean, a regionally popular stand-up, a local bluegrass music group called Three on a

String, and the Naked Cowboy. "Naked" was a guy who passed through Birmingham, playing his guitar and singing, wearing nothing but his tighty-whiteys and a cowboy hat. He was an unknown then, but is a fixture now in New York City's Times Square.

We also had friend-of-the-show Kevin Derryberry, who was just beginning what would become a very successful career in Christian music after playing in several popular rock bands. His testimony is powerful, and we still love having him on the show, but nobody knew him then. Nobody except the people who listened to Rick and Bubba.

I had a band then called Mr. Lucky, but we rarely played and certainly had no hit songs. We were ready to do a set that night—even if

The show gave me a much larger platform to go back and live the rock star dream

we didn't have a chance to practice much—and were about as close to a headline act as could be found on the bill for Fat Fest I.

I remember distinctly driving to the amphitheater that afternoon with absolutely no idea how many people would show up. There were ten thousand seats in the place, and it would be disheartening if they were mostly empty. Still, we had decided that we were going to put on a bang-up show for a hundred folks if that was all there was, and it would be one of the best shows that tiny little crowd had ever seen.

Of course, I also remember praying that at least a hundred would show up.

My heart raced when I got within a mile of the place and there was a traffic jam from cars exiting off I-65. I later learned that all the area hotels were full, that people had driven hundreds of miles and spent the night to attend Fat Fest.

Tony Ruffino, the local promoter and then owner of the amphitheater, met me at the stage gate. "Did you do this?" he asked. Tony had made a good living out of estimating the draw of various acts from the Rolling Stones to Led Zeppelin. He was in disbelief. "Did all these people show up to watch a radio show?"

I could only shrug. The best estimate we had of the crowd that night was between five thousand and seven thousand people. That many people to "watch" a radio show! Tony told us it wasn't the typical amphitheater crowd either. He later reported that they sold five thousand hot dogs but only two beers!

We did Fat Fest for five straight years, and each was just as successful as the others. It was the listeners who made it so. We never had a big-name act. It was always people from the show and friends of the show. For example, we had country singer Keith Anderson on one of the shows before he had even signed his first record deal. He had visited the show and sung some of the songs he had written, and the listeners liked him. I think we paid him six hundred dollars. He went on to have a string of top-ten songs and gold albums.

This is one of our many projects, a giant hot dog that shoots T-shirts into the crowd

We elected not to do more Fat Fests after the fifth one. Bubba and I have this theory we call "the Circle." The radio show is at the center of that circle, the goose that laid the golden egg. We can get involved with other things—Fat Fest, public speaking, writing books, Bubba's infatuation with tennis—but when it becomes too much, we pull back within the circle. We can't allow anything to distract us from doing the best radio show we can do every morning. We owe it to our listeners, our sponsors, and our syndicated stations not to let other projects detract from the goose in the middle of that circle.

The truth is, WYSF still needed some help, even as the *Rick and Bubba Show* thrived. Like the Q when we first got there, the station had fallen greatly since Mark and Brian ("Come, money, come. Come, money, come") were doing mornings there. Still, Davis took the big-dollar risk, and then he stepped out of our way and gave us plenty of room to roam. We will be forever grateful to him and the company.

That's one reason why we were about as happy for him as we were for the rest of the people on the show and ourselves when the first ratings book came out. The *Rick and Bubba Show*—the little radio show that was "about everything," just the opposite of *Seinfeld*, a show "about nothing"—was number one across the board in the Birmingham market. That was a triumphant day when Davis burst into the studio with the numbers scrawled on a scrap of paper, grinning from ear to ear.

We did not gloat . . . much. Oh, we let some of the others who had openly doubted us—questioned us as well as the power and loyalty of our audience—know how we felt about this God-given victory. But we gave credit to our listeners, our sponsors, and our Lord. We also knew we would have to work harder now. As difficult as it was to get to the top of the mountain, it would be even more work to stay on the summit and defend the territory we had captured.

The war was on!

The Rick and Bubba merchandise was going great by this time. Our "best of" CDs were popular. Charity events were packed. People were yelling, "Rick and Bubba!" when they saw either of us in the grocery store or at the ballpark. I think we were both starting to feel like stars for the first time in our lives. For the seven years that we were at Dick Broadcasting, we were consistently number one. Station revenues were spectacular and commercial time on the show was usually sold out well in advance.

We figured as long as we kept it real on the air, and as long as we evolved the show naturally, not forcing anything, we would be okay. We were sure we had a feel for what we needed to do. The listeners trusted us to do the right thing, to be ourselves, to have a show to which they could relate. Trusted us to do a show they could feel comfortable listening to with the kids in the car on the way to school. It was a show about our lives, but it was, at the same time, a show about their lives, about things similar to what happened to them and their families, only much funnier and louder.

At one point the station ownership realized that the listening audience on WYSF dropped off dramatically after 10:00 a.m., when the *Rick and Bubba Show* went off the air. They tried different personalities, local and nationally syndicated, tinkered with the music and the station's format, and did all the usual tricks to try to improve the ratings for the rest of the day. We braced ourselves for the same logic that our former employers used on us: we were too different from the rest of the broadcast day, and we were so popular that we were ruining the station.

To their credit, they didn't make that leap. In fact, they eventually got around to asking us what we thought they should do—change musical formats? Hire a truly high-powered personality for the afternoon drive segment? Bubba and I were not bashful. We suggested they put a replay of each day's *Rick and Bubba Show* on the air in afternoon drive time. The Q had, at one point, replayed our show in the evenings and made money with that time period for the first time in the station's history. Even 94.5 WYSF had begun replaying a recorded portion of our show in the evening hours, and ratings and revenue had gone up for those couple of hours.

But to have the same show rebroadcast in afternoon drive, in the second most important part of the station's broadcast day? That was unheard-of.

They finally grew desperate enough to give it a try, though. You know what? It worked. The afternoon replay was soon consistently in the top five of all stations in Birmingham for that time period. Once again, we didn't gloat—at least, not much.

Bill and I still had hopes of syndicating the show to more than the couple of markets where we were already. Once we were number one in the ratings in our home city and the rates that could be charged for commercials on the show had topped out, there was nowhere else to go. We knew that what we did on the air would play just as well in other cities as it did in Birmingham. That was especially true of those markets around the South, regardless of size and "sophistication."

Bubba had already begun working on installing and hooking up a high-quality telephone network. On our own, and relying on some contacts we had in the business, we managed to pick up a dozen or so other stations over the next year. Still, we just couldn't seem to get on the big signals in the larger markets like Atlanta, Charlotte, Memphis, or Nashville.

Our operations manager at WYSF, Kerry Lambert, who did many things around the cluster of stations already, was given yet another job. He was told to try to help, along with Bubba and me, to syndicate the *Rick and Bubba Show*. We were following the lead of Dick Broadcasting, our partners in the effort, and they were opposed to the usual method for stations to pay for syndicated programming. It is called barter—making the show available at little or no charge to station partners in exchange for advertising time on the affiliates that could be sold by the network. The demands on Kerry's time—and he did work hard for us—and the lack of a barter setup hindered us from being able to accomplish what we hoped to do. Syndication and spreading the show to other markets, even in the light of our success in Birmingham, proved to be elusive.

Anyone listening to the show over the years, or who hears the range of bits on our CDs or "best of" shows, can tell that the *Rick and Bubba Show* did not stay the same. Part of the evolution during these years involved our talking more and more openly about our faith. It had been a part of the show since the beginning. We talked and laughed about things that happened in church or at church-related events, and we invited our ministers and Sunday school teachers to be guests on the show.

We figured if the show was about us, about our lives, and if our faith was real, then it had to be a part of what we did on the air. Still, we weren't heavy-handed about it. I will admit that even Bubba and

I sometimes worried a bit about trying to bring religion to a secular radio show and whether it fit with all the craziness we did on the air. Did we really want to mess with a winning formula and allow more of our beliefs to come through?

I was going through a change in my own spiritual life, too. See, I was always a "cultural Christian," even during the times when I was absorbed in a terrible lifestyle. I went to church and did what I thought Christians were supposed to do before I went away to college. After that, I did neither. I had a Bible, but I rarely read it. I certainly didn't study it and try to understand what God wanted me to do in this life.

When we were still in Gadsden, I woke up one day and realized that I had to be a better father to my two children, Brandi and Blake. I would need to be a better husband for Sherri once we married. That was when I truly began contemplating a stronger walk with God, but I still didn't know how to do it.

A series of events leading up to my marriage to Sherri really sealed the deal. I was still basking in my success of winning her over so very publicly. I loved her deeply and wanted nothing more than to share the rest of my life with her. And—amazingly enough—Sherri felt the same about me.

She and I made an appointment to meet with our minister, a wonderful man of God, Rev. Rick Cagle. We wanted to tell him of our devotion to each other, that we were going to be married, and that we wanted him to perform the ceremony in his church. Brother Cagle was a fan of the show, a good man, and Sherri and I could think of nobody better to unite us in holy matrimony.

He had a shocking reaction at our meeting. Brother Rick looked me squarely in the eye and said, "No. I won't marry you. You are lost."

Just as my mother had once done, someone else was watching my lifestyle and questioning my salvation.

I was stunned. I admit that his blunt words crushed me. How could someone I trusted and respected so much flatly refuse to do something that was so important to me? But—after some heart-to-hearts with him—the frankness of what he was telling me finally hit home.

Brother Cagle knew something I didn't even know about myself: I still wasn't truly convicted. He certainly knew from talking with me—from watching me—that I still wasn't sure about what the *holy* in "holy matrimony" really meant.

The same day Brother Rick told me about his doubts about my faith, Sherri and I talked about what he'd said. Neither of us fully understood. When I got home that evening, I looked all over until I found my Bible. I'm not sure what I hoped to find there, but something told me God would show me the words. Oh, I knew Genesis was the first book, Revelation the last, and I probably could've quoted John 3:16, but that was about it.

When I opened the Bible, it fell to the book of James, chapter 4, verses 7 and 8. It said, as if it was written just for Rick Burgess to read at that very moment in time, "Submit yourselves, then, to God. Resist the devil, and he will flee from you. Come near to God and he will come near to you. Wash your hands, you sinners, and purify your hearts, you double-minded" (NIV).

There it was. It clicked.

The words on that page were meant for us as surely as if James had us in mind when he wrote them. Brother Cagle counseled with us, prayed with us, and only after he was sure that Sherri and I understood the "holy" part of a sanctified marriage, he proudly and eagerly performed the ceremony.

I was convicted!

As I mentioned before, there have been many times when Bubba and I have wondered if we should allow our faith to be so much a part of the show. Maybe, we reasoned, we should go to Christian radio instead. There have been many folks—including some we trust implicitly and who have our best interests at heart—who have told us it is a mistake to make our beliefs such a big, public part of what we do, on and off the air. We would eventually get the same kind of negative input when we began allowing our conservative political beliefs to emerge.

Rick and Bubba on a book tour

But we always come right back to a basic fact: this is who we are. And the show is, always has been, and always will be about who we are.

We continued to have ministers on the show and featured Christian music at times. We began talking about some of the crazy and dangerous things our government was doing to us. So far, thank the Lord, our listenership has only continued to grow.

See, we are convinced that God gave us this platform, that His hand is guiding us, and so long as we take His lead, He continues to bless us. If we are doing this to glorify Him, how could it possibly be the wrong thing to do? Are we going to listen to those broadcast consultants instead of the Lord?

Everything was working so well. Our success seemed to be confirming that we were doing the right thing bringing to the show our faith, our politics, our love for hunting, and all the other things that made us so radically different from everything else on the dial. Despite what the experts and consultants predicted, the show prospered. My marriage was solid, and Sherri had quickly become a wonderful stepmom for my two children from my previous marriage. Both kids went to church with us. Maybe best of all, with our jobs secure at a supportive radio station, God was about to bless Sherri and me with a new baby.

Sherri's pregnancy progressed normally, despite all the drama early on when Bubba and I were in such limbo about the future of the show. She was so excited about her first pregnancy and proud to be having our son. Then her water broke in the middle of the night, and she went into labor. We rushed to the hospital, but the doctor told us it would be hours before she delivered, based on the intensity of her labor. We called all the kinfolk and told them we were at the hospital. I suggested they take their time getting there, that Sherri had not progressed very far, and it would be a while before Brooks—the "B" name we had chosen—would make his grand entrance into the world.

Shortly after we arrived at the hospital, the doctor gave Sherri a drug to help speed up her labor just a bit. Moments after the injection, Sherri realized she was in trouble. She had a severe reaction to the drug and immediately had a massive labor contraction. The expression on the nurse's face confirmed that something serious was going on. So did the fact that she immediately paged the doctor.

"Mr. Burgess, we are going to have to take the baby by Caesarian section," he told me. "There is almost certainly a ruptured placenta. The baby and your wife are both in danger. We'll do the best we can."

I could not believe it. Up until a few minutes before, everything in my life was going so great. God was answering our prayers for a smooth delivery and a healthy son.

Now, in an instant, I was in real danger of losing my wife and our unborn baby boy.

"What can I do?" I asked the doctor, feeling as helpless as I ever had in my life.

"Pray," he said. "Pray."

You can be certain that is exactly what I did.

Standing just outside the operating room door, I know my lips were moving as I watched the doctor and his team literally take our son. He was big, bloody, and blue when the obstetrician held him up for me to see. Was a human baby supposed to look like that?

I instinctively let out a whoop when the doc gave me a big

thumbs-up. Our boy was okay! Brooks Burgess had made a rather dramatic entrance into the world!

But what about Sherri? *Lord, please let her be okay.*

It seemed like hours, but it was probably only a few minutes that they worked over her. They had, at this point, forgotten all about me. I figured as long as they were doing things, she was alive. And I prayed even harder, cried without shame, and pleaded with God to let her survive. Survive to be the mother I knew she would be for our child, even as that newborn kid wailed and screeched like crazy.

Finally the doctor gave me another thumbs-up, the most beautiful sign I had ever seen. He walked over to the door to tell me that Sherri had lost a lot of blood but she would be okay. Both mother and baby would be fine.

I thanked him—and might well have kissed him if he hadn't turned and run the other way—then started out to the waiting room where the rest of the family had hastily assembled. I couldn't wait to tell everyone what a wonderful thing our Lord had done for us that early morning.

"God is great!" I said aloud, not caring who heard me. "God is great!"

The hallway was noisy, nurses and hospital staff and family members hustling from one patient to another, but several people smiled at me. A couple of them patted me on the shoulder. Some looked the other way, avoiding eye contact with what was obviously some "religious nut."

Then, even above the racket in the hospital hallway, I distinctly heard a powerful whisper, a voice speaking to me.

"What if they had died?"

I stopped and looked around me. No one was near me at the moment. No one was talking to me. A chill ran up my spine.

"What?" I asked.

"What if they had died? Would I be any less great?"

I knew then that it was God. Would my faith have survived if He had taken away from me either or both of the people I loved so very much?

I admit that I didn't have the answer to His question. But as I steadied myself and made my way on out into the waiting room to deliver the wonderful news to anxious family members, a cold thought gripped me: He was teaching me something. There would come a time when I would face an even stronger test of my conviction and faith.

No telling when or what, but it would certainly come.

14 The Eye That Does Not Blink

I—Bubba—would never claim to be an old hand at television, but I did work at Channel 40 in Anniston as a technical director. While I was there, I actually applied for and received a license or two for TV stations. Then, you remember, I was a sales exec at the Gadsden television station for about a minute and a half. Since the beginning, though, it's been radio that has most strongly caught and held my interest.

My partner, Rick, has even less experience with the big eye. Granted, we did do a short-lived television show together when we were in Gadsden. That was a lot of fun, and people still talk about some of the things we did. The truth is, though, TV is one medium that can cramp our style big-time. We would have to come up with things to do that played better on video, get a camera crew together, cameras, microphones, lights and sets, go on location, shoot, edit, and finally go to air.

With radio we just open the microphone and talk about whatever we want to. It's so easy to pick up the telephone and put listeners and contributors on the air immediately.

So imagine our surprise when we got the chance to do television again, two hours a day, five days a week, live and unedited.

Rick and I would soon realize that this was one eye that never blinked.

Turner Broadcasting has always been an innovator. The company was started by Ted Turner, the Atlanta mogul, who inherited a failing UHF television station with no—and I mean *no*—viewers at all. But you have to admit that Ted is a visionary, even if his politics and choices in wives are sometimes suspect. He knew cable television would soon be hungry for programming beyond just rebroadcasting the signals of local TV stations, as it was originally created to do.

He bought up the rights for hours and hours of family-friendly programming and put it on his lowly little Channel 17. Then he offered the broadcast to cable operators all over the country as a new channel. He even paid them to carry his channel, and that got their attention in a hurry. He knew that if he congregated enough viewers on the rebroadcast of his station on those cable channels out there, he could sell advertising to sponsors who didn't care if viewers were seeing the shows and ads over the air or via cable. Eyeballs are eyeballs.

Ted also began buying sports franchises, such as my beloved Atlanta Braves, and putting those games on the newly christened Superstation. And then he created a twenty-four-hour-a-day news channel, Cable News Network (CNN), the TNN network, Turner Classic Movies, and more.

One of Turner's newest ventures was a cable channel called Turner South. The company was determined to put as much exclusive programming on the channel as they could, so long as it had a Southern accent, and to make it a force on cable systems all over the region. Somehow, the folks at Turner Broadcasting caught wind of a little radio show over yonder in Birmingham, Alabama. Out of the blue we were approached about allowing them to telecast two hours of our show each day by simply putting cameras in the control room. They envisioned a "visual radio show."

Not only were we flattered; we were certain it was a can't-miss deal! We considered ourselves a visual show already. After all, we had Jim the Crazy Sign Man, we "showed" videos and episodes from the previous night's TV shows, and we had in-studio entertainers. Plus we were already holding lawn mower races with NASCAR stars at the "wheel," tossing frozen turkeys for prizes, and having Halloween costume contests in the parking lot. At our studios on a bluff overlooking downtown Birmingham, we had imported a discarded statue of Big Boy, salvaged from the rapidly disappearing restaurant chain whose symbol he was, and we did all sorts of events out there around him. We even held a wedding there, giving a play-by-play of the ceremony—on the radio.

Television would be a natural, so we told Turner to go ahead and turn on the cameras. Dick Broadcasting was all for it, too. After all, it was a great promotional avenue for the show. They even made sure the new studios they were building for us at the time would accommodate the needs of the TV side. Maybe they went too far there. To allow the cameras to be located where Turner wanted, they positioned our broadcast console and our seats much too close to the back wall of the studio, especially for a couple of fat guys—sexy or not. We had a running joke about the huge studio, but it was a fat man's squeeze for us to get around to the audio board and microphones.

Rick and Bubba shoot TV promos for Rick and Bubba the TV show on Turner South

Regardless, we dubbed our new digs "the Red Velvet Lounge," and it was a dream come true for a couple of guys who had broadcast from some of the dingiest closets you could ever imagine. Just the equipment alone was a gadget guy's paradise. The cameras, wireless microphones, computers, and other stuff that went into that studio made it like Christmas morning every day when I got to the studio. It was a long way from those little walkie-talkies with the screw lodged in the coil!

I will admit that the first few days we were on Turner South, we looked like possums caught in the headlights. We couldn't forget that thousands of people were now watching us on TV, as well as all those others who were listening in on the radio, and we found ourselves staring into the cameras that were bracketed to the walls. We had to be careful about what facial expressions we made, even more careful about where we scratched and what we said off-mike, just for those lip readers out there in television land.

We made no wardrobe changes. I continued to wear football jerseys and shorts most days, even in winter, just as I always had. And so did Rick. Our wives did encourage us to shave every day. That had never been a problem on the radio.

Still, even though we were determined not to allow the cameras to affect what we did and change the tone of the show, we couldn't help playing to the lenses. Suddenly we were aware that we were trying to catch glimpses of ourselves in the monitors, to see how we looked on TV.

An even bigger problem was one we had first experienced when we started syndicating to other radio stations: we had to time everything to the TV schedule. No matter how great a conversation or bit might be going on, when the time came, we had to bail for commercials at what is called a "hard break." And we couldn't afford to run out of anything to do on the show, either. If we reached a natural stopping point, we couldn't just arbitrarily go to commercial break if it wasn't time for TV or the network to take a break.

We also caught ourselves saving the best guests and the funniest material for the TV hours. We knew we were shortchanging the listeners who had supported us but who could not stay around until the cameras were turned on each morning.

This television thing was also a lot more work. More, I think, than we'd bargained for. It reminded me of the days back in the beginning when we did the show in the morning, a remote broadcast at some car dealership in the afternoon, and then *Pigskin Roundup* at night. Now, once we were off the air, we had to stick around and shoot promotional announcements for future shows that would be run on the network. We had to go to Atlanta for meetings and more video shoots, too.

In fact, this TV thing required an inordinate number of meetings and memos!

When we did any remote broadcasts or outside bits, we had to consider the planning and logistics for TV. We had to figure the complexity and cost of having television cameras, lights, a crew, and more along for the ride. No longer could we just take a microphone and remote link (often just a cell phone) out to some location and be on the air for radio.

Things came to a head when we were broadcasting from a big barbecue festival in Memphis. After a lot of work—and many, many meetings and memos—things were going along pretty well with the event on both radio and TV. Then, suddenly, storms threatened our open broadcast position. No problem, we figured. We could take the radio gear and cameras into a nearby tent during a break and not miss a beat.

The television folks said no, that we would have to stay where we were and try to get enough umbrellas to keep the radio equipment and us dry. There wasn't enough light in the tent for TV, so we had to stay put, out in the elements. The cameras were covered already. We argued that if the radio gear got wet, we might well be off the air. And by the way, radio was what paid the bills. We could not risk losing the stations on the network just so TV viewers would have better lighting.

That was when we made the big decision to do our show the way we had always done it, and TV could just be there to shoot it as it happened. Rick and I are both still convinced that made the show even better, for both radio and Turner South.

Don't get me wrong; we really enjoyed our relationship with Turner. They believed in what we were doing and promoted the show and us heavily. They were nothing but professional all the way and made the show appear to be bigger by far than it really was. That fit something we had been doing all along, since Rick first called his show the *Morning Extravaganza*. That's show business!

So we were really sad the day we learned that Fox Television had purchased Turner South and was going to turn it into an all-sports channel. They were up-front with us and told us the cameras in the Red Velvet Lounge would go dark soon. It was a good run, and despite those hassles, we thoroughly enjoyed it. Viewers and listeners still tell us that they did too.

Those seven years with Dick Broadcasting and Citadel Broadcasting, who eventually bought most of the Dick stations, was a wonderful time for us. The show was prospering, our families were growing, we were having more fun than anybody should be allowed to have, and we were getting paid handsomely for it.

The show was a very good thing for Dick Broadcasting, too. When Citadel galloped in and paid Mr. Dick and his family many millions of dollars for WYSF and most of his other stations, Rick sent our old bosses a note. He told them that we would expect a check with lots of commas on the amount line in appreciation of what we did to help get him that nice payday. To his credit, he and his company did give us—along with many others who had been instrumental in the company's success—a check. Not with what I would call lots of commas in the amount, but we did appreciate it very much.

Still, with a new and massive conglomerate as our new owners, we weren't sure what the future held for the *Rick and Bubba Show*. We just kept doing what we'd been doing for the past dozen years—being ourselves, having fun, keeping it real.

We had formally incorporated the show way back when we were still in Gadsden, keeping syndication and merchandising separate from the deal with the station. That allowed us to partner eventually with an outside company to help syndicate the show to more markets, and especially in those midsized markets where we knew our show would play well. It seemed as if every Monday morning we were welcoming aboard a new affiliate from somewhere.

"Give us a month," we would tell them. "Just give us a month before you pull the plug."

We knew for the first few weeks the station owners would be shocked by the kind of show they had contracted to put on their air.

They would have their friends in the radio business questioning their sanity as well. The listeners, too, might wonder what kind of brawl they had just wandered into the middle of, and some might protest losing whatever had been on the station before we got there.

But then, if the owners paid attention and gave the listeners the opportunity to hear what we were doing, they would realize they had not lost their minds by signing on the two sexiest fat men alive.

"Don't listen to your friends at the country club," we told them. "Ignore the ridicule you'll get at the broadcasters' meeting. For goodness' sake, don't pay any attention to the media critics from the newspaper or the research-loving program directors and radio consultant goobs. Listen to your listeners. Your listeners and your advertisers. They'll tell you how things are going. Then, if it's not working, you can pull us off."

As Rick has noted, none of the competitors knew how to come at us. The radio industry had changed. Since most radio stations were either running programming from a computerized automation system—a jukebox—at night and on weekends, or riding a satellite feed, there was no "farm team" of young talent coming up the pipeline. There was no time when new, hopeful personalities could develop their acts in the wee hours when few people would be listening. Young talent was going elsewhere, not to an underpaid job in local radio. In bigger markets, stations began looking to hire stand-up comedians and put them on the air.

They were comedians and they knew how to be funny, the managers figured. And it was all about being funny, right?

Trouble was, those guys typically had a set routine they did night in and night out onstage. Since the audiences were different every night, they simply did the same jokes every time. With radio, they could only use a made-up joke or bit once or twice to keep it fresh. And they had to entertain five days a week, three or four hours a day, not for a quick half-hour set. They typically worked without restrictions in the comedy clubs, and many of them did not know how to be funny without being vulgar.

Besides, when they were on the radio, there was no laughter from the audience to spur them on, to let them know how their material was playing. I think that's why so many of these shows have newspeople and interns and whoever else they can round up to be in the studio, forcing uproarious laughter, just so the audience listening at home or in their cars or at work know when they are supposed to laugh.

It was also difficult for the other stations, their programmers, and their consultants to come up with a way to combat our little show. They continued to make snide comments about us, but they couldn't figure out a way to "out–Rick-and-Bubba" Rick and Bubba, even if they wanted to.

I tell you this in all sincerity. I prayed every day that they never would get any smarter.

15 The Broadcast Plaza and Teleport

We have asked our listeners—bless 'em—to follow us up and down the dial a few times already. We hoped we never would have to ask again. One day they might suddenly decide, "Hey, those fat boys are just greedy! I'm staying here after they're gone, and I'm going to see if there is something coming along that's better than Bubba quoting Shakespeare and Rick singing along with the bumper music."

But there are perfectly good reasons for every move Bill and I have made. Believe me when I say this: a lot of it has to do with those listeners.

If we can have the freedom to do what we feel we need to do, to say the things we want to say, to talk about Jesus

Christ right out there in the open, and if we can open a microphone and say that we think the Democrats are leading us down the rosy path to socialism, then it benefits our audience when we do it. If we can have a more powerful signal, an even bigger platform from which to serve, better equipment, more promotion, book deals, syndication, and more, then it's in all our interests to mosey on back up to another spot on the radio dial.

Sure, money and security for our families are part of it. But sometimes we have to take a stand and go elsewhere if it gives us a better opportunity to do what we do for the people we do it for.

It's not for our own glory or gratification or to stoke our egos. It's because we believe we have something to say that our audience needs to hear. That they want to hear. And we are more than willing to listen to them if they have opposing viewpoints.

Still, it's scary every time we've made a move from one station to another. That's especially true when everything is going pretty well where we are, but something tells us it's time to ease on down the road. Our families are growing and depend on us for so much. The rest of the people who are a part of the show, and who now have families of their own, are depending on our success and on Bubba and me making the right choices.

It gives us pause. It puts us on our knees, praying for guidance.

Sometimes, though, you just have to step out of the airplane without a parachute and have every confidence that you will land in a mattress factory.

———

So it was that after two contract renewals with Dick and Citadel, we were coming up on another negotiation. After the nerve-racking experience in David Marsh's office that eventually led us to our seven years at 94.5 WYSF, neither Bubba nor I was too excited about another negotiation. Even so, as we approached the end of our contract, we decided to test the waters, even though we were happy at Citadel and thrilled with how well the show was doing.

Something—a small but insistent voice inside—told us that there was more out there, an opportunity to do more with the direction the show was heading. Besides, if Citadel really wanted us to stay, they could certainly make that happen.

We were gratified by the offers we received. Finally, it appeared that others, including the very biggest radio operators, were impressed enough with what we had accomplished that they were willing to pay to have us do it over at their place.

Then there came that fateful day when we were down to making a decision. For some reason, the head of Citadel was stuck on a number and refused to budge. It was not that far from the best offers from the others, but there was absolutely no interest in matching the other offers. The CEO himself threw out a figure and said, "Not a penny more." There was no doubt in our minds that he meant it.

We had to consider if it was better to stay where we were for less or jump and try to land safely with another operator. And remember, we had to consider the employees of Rick and Bubba Incorporated and their families, the syndication company and stations who had cast their lot with us on the network, and the sponsors who had been with us for so long. Not to mention my growing brood of kids. Sherri and I had three by this time, and along with my two with my first wife, that gave us five. Betty and Bill were now blessed with an expanding family too. Hunter and Katelyn had joined the Bussey Bunch by then.

Would we get across the street and discover the new bosses wanted us to hush up the religion and the politics and the other things we believed were important? Would they want us to stop the things that mattered to us and to the people who listened to us?

I would like to say there was no emotion involved and that having our current station owner refuse to match the other offers didn't bother us. That wouldn't be true, though. Honestly, it was not all about the money. We wanted freedom and a facility that would allow us to serve our affiliates and sponsors better. It also needed to be set up for television since we always intended to get back into that medium as well. It was disappointing to us that the current station ownership seemed more determined to win the war of negotiation than to make us feel like they wanted us to stay.

There was one other factor. We'd been mightily impressed by the interest from one of the groups with whom we'd been talking. The other station owners kept asking us what we wanted. We kept telling them to make us an offer, but they insisted on talking in circles and generalities and balked at putting anything specific into writing.

178

The good folks from Cox Communications in Atlanta not only made solid commitments and put them on paper for us to consider; they talked dollars and facilities. They even took us to a location south of Birmingham, where they proposed building us new studios and gave us a tour of the building. They pointed out where the on-air equipment would go, where each of our offices would be, where the seats would be installed for visitors to come in and watch us live, and the area where musical guests would be able to perform. They were even going to put in a full kitchen so we could keep warm all that free food for which we continued to beg.

We made several trips to Atlanta to meet with the Cox folks. On one trip we sat in a conference room alone with Neal Bortz, the highly successful Libertarian talk show host. He had started on the big Cox station in Atlanta, WSB-AM, and was later syndicated nationally by

Rick and Bubba with Neal Bortz

the company. We asked him to tell us honestly about these people with whom we were considering hooking up.

"All radio people are slime," he told us with a straight face. "But these folks are the least slimy of any of them."

Finally, with that hardy endorsement from Bortz, Bill and I—after a lot of prayer and discussion with each other and our wives—decided to take the plunge with Cox. We would be the new morning show on WZZK-FM, a truly legendary country music radio station in Birmingham. They were the ones who just beat us after the Q moved to Birmingham. With a history of country dominance or not, they had no qualms about our not playing much music, or about our using everything from rock to rap for bumper music, or playing Christian artists.

Again we were lame ducks, but once more we did our very best to make those last days on WYSF as good as we could. We had no animosity for anyone there. They had been great to work with. Besides, we had several more weeks to go on our contract before we were scheduled to move over to WZZK. The engineers at the new station were still in the process of hooking up a temporary studio while they were building the new digs south of town, wiring up for the switchover for the syndicated stations, and even arranging our toll-free line, 877-WE BE BIG, to ring at the new place once we were over there.

Sherri and I had planned a vacation to Disney World, so we went ahead, loading up our litter of young 'uns and heading south. Speedy, as usual, was there to play "best of Rick and Bubba" bits on the air. Then we figured we would come back from vacation, do a farewell week, and go on the air on WZZK the next Monday after that.

Nope. From the very top of the organization, Citadel sent word to the folks in Birmingham that we were done there.

Speedy got in touch with me when I was on Space Mountain, waiting in line for that wild ride, to tell me we were off the air. Citadel had pulled the plug. They had also pulled the plug on the affiliated stations, putting on a totally new morning show without any warning, pairing up a couple of personalities from their other stations. Though innocent in the whole thing, those guys had already experienced the wrath of our listening audience simply because they were not Rick and Bubba.

Rick and Bubba on location, sacrificing at a beautiful beach resort

We had hasty discussions with the folks at Cox. They didn't have our temporary studio ready yet, but they'd see what they could do. Within a few days they had rigged us a console, computers, microphones, and

181

the other equipment we needed to broadcast. It was nowhere near as sumptuous as the Red Velvet Lounge that we were leaving, nor did it even vaguely resemble the "Broadcast Plaza and Teleport"—our affectionate name for our new studios that were under construction—but we were on the air.

Sort of.

It would take us several days to get used to the jury-rigged setup and the cramped quarters, but we sucked it up and did what we had to do. The Cox engineers had pulled off a miracle, and we were not about to fuss because it wasn't the perfect operation. Of course, we found humor in the situation, too.

Rick and Bubba were back on the air at a new spot on the dial, doing whatever it was that we did, but without the serious hiatus there could have been. The listeners told us we hadn't lost them, that they'd followed us without hesitation. That only spurred us to do even better for them and for the new group owners who had placed so much confidence in us and the unorthodox radio show we did.

Despite the suddenness of the transition, and no matter all the worry about making a move after so long at the other place, the show seemed to get back to normal quickly. We were tossing turkeys at Thanksgiving and challenging the People for Ethical Treatment of Animals, gigging the global warming movement and recapping *American Idol*.

In short, everything was going great once again for the *Rick and Bubba Show*.

Little did we know then what lay directly ahead of us. The test God had whispered to me the night Brooks was born? It was looming, and when it came, nothing would ever be the same. Not for me, not for my family, and not for the show.

And, thank the Lord, not for the millions who so deeply shared the experience with us.

16 "Hey, You're Broadcasting!"

We expose ourselves every morning on a nationally syndicated radio show. Whoa! You know what I mean. Rick and I enjoy hunting, so we talk about hunting. I play tennis. Win or lose, we talk about the previous weekend's match. We have talked about Betty mopping naked and Rick and Sherri doing man/ wife things on a cruise ship, unaware that the blinds were open to the main deck.

There is no doubt about where we stand on our faith. Our politics are right out there, like 'em or not. Hunter and Katelyn, my kids, have grown up having their daddy talk about them and their potty training and teething and strikeouts and—praise

God!—their acceptance of Jesus and baptism, all on the radio and in front of millions of strangers.

If Rick or Speedy or Greg or I are ever in a bad mood, we have to get over it before 6:00 a.m. Central time, or that comes across over the air too. If it's a miserable day—raining, dark, and dreary—we have to remember the sun may be shining somewhere else that the show reaches. We can't let that affect how we sound.

If something is going on in the country, though, we have to acknowledge it. It may be something people are talking about already or that affects a lot of our audience, whether it's that terrible, off-key singer with the orange hair on *American Idol* or the Democrats doing something that will cost us taxpayers another trillion dollars.

If something is happening in our families—good, bad, or indifferent—we necessarily have to include it as part of the show too. Rick said it best earlier. *Seinfeld* is a show about nothing. *Rick and Bubba* is a show about everything.

That must always be the case, even when "everything" is tragic beyond belief.

People—and especially those who still do not understand why the *Rick and Bubba Show* works at all—sometimes have trouble with us talking about things like hunting, playing tennis, going to church. But we can no more ignore all that than we could stop eating gravy and biscuits.

It is us. And us is the show.

Betty and I were on vacation one time and decided to play some tennis. No, I still don't know why. I had, prior to that turning point in my athletic life, much rather hurl a baseball at somebody who is trying to hit it back at me with a bat than try to steer it at them with a snowshoe. Still, the mood hit us, so we ran out to Walmart and bought a couple of ten-dollar tennis rackets. Then we got out there on the tennis court as if we knew what we were doing.

Not that I am competitive by nature or anything, but I took no mercy and beat Betty solidly that fateful day. I had no idea I had unleashed the beast.

Now, if you know Betty Bussey, you know that such humiliation does not get her down and depressed. Instead, it spurs her to greatness. It was no time before she not only began pounding me into the ground, but she'd soon moved on and was playing on a state championship tennis team.

Me? I still play. And I am getting better, despite two knee surgeries and hours of physical therapy.

That's typical of us, though. Rick and I don't do anything halfhearted, whether it be sports, radio, or an all-you-can-eat buffet. Tennis is now a big part of my life, and even though Rick maintains I've gone too far and it now dominates me, we still talk about it on the show on a regular basis. How could we not?

Hunting is another example. I grew up hunting, and so did Rick. It was always a great way to get into the outdoors, although sometimes, when it was cold enough to give Satan frostbite, I had to wonder why I had not stayed in that nice, warm bed. We really enjoy shooting furry critters and doing it with people we genuinely enjoy hanging out with. I even went so far as to invest in a plot of land—named "the Bubbarosa" by my radio partner—just so I would have a place to hunt with my friends and family.

Whatever went on in the deer stand or on the bass boat was fair game for the next day's *Rick and Bubba Show*. Apparently nobody since Marconi invented radio had ever discussed the previous weekend's deer hunt on morning radio. Or at least it appeared that way if you listened to some of the squawking we heard. It wasn't long before we heard from the People for Ethical Treatment of Animals (PETA). The only thing is that they're so far out of this solar system with their ideas and tactics that they're not really all that much fun to debate.

All right, if the show is driven by our lives and by the events that our listeners and we commonly experience, what do we do when tragedy happens? Hopefully, we do what we always do. We talk about it from our own perspective.

There was that morning in September 2001. I don't remember what we were ranting and raving about, but we were talking with Mark Prater, a local television weatherman who was a regular on the program at the time. He suddenly said, "Oh, by the way, the World Trade Center is on fire!"

We looked up at one of the television monitors in the studio. Sure enough, they were showing a big building with smoke billowing from it. A fire?

Then I could tell that it was one of the World Trade Center towers. Rick and I had already made several trips to New York City as part of the show and had been inside that very building. Shoot, we'd had lunch at a restaurant at the very top.

Roxanne, the newsperson on duty at the station that day, came into the studio to join us as we discussed what we were seeing. She reported that first accounts said a twin-engine airplane had crashed into the World Trade Center.

Comedian Mickey Dean, also a show regular, suddenly got uncharacteristically serious.

"No small airplane caused all that damage," he noted, looking at the gaping hole in the structure.

And just then, a second airplane hit the other tower.

"We're under attack!" Speedy called out.

We still could not believe what we were seeing, but, like the rest of the world, we were watching it as it happened. Naturally we did what we do and spoke spontaneously—speculating, reporting, reacting.

Rick was the first to mention that the airplanes had to have been under terrorist control. Others came up with some rather wild ideas about what was happening, but Rick and I tried not to go too far afield. When someone told us the White House had been attacked, we urged everyone not to believe everything they heard, to wait until we knew the facts for certain.

We did know one thing for sure. Something unprecedented was taking place.

It seemed to have all the earmarks of a terrorist attack, and we said so. It was obviously an act of war, and we acknowledged that too.

We ran with it. It is like the title of one of our "best of" CDs: sometimes we forget and have to remind ourselves that "Hey, we're broadcasting!"

We used television audio, the video we could see, and reports from

189

the wire services to keep our audience updated. Listeners called in with their own news, some gleaned from the media, others after talking with friends or relatives who were in New York City at the time, including some inside the Twin Towers. Another show regular, TV sportscaster Jim Dunaway, who did sports reports for the show, chimed in with what he was hearing at the TV station where he worked. Roxanne jumped in to say the Associated Press was relaying that at least one of the planes that struck the World Trade Center had reportedly been hijacked earlier in the morning.

Then, a few minutes later, the AP reported a plane had just crashed into the Pentagon and that all aircraft had been ordered to land immediately. No aircraft would be authorized to take off until further notice.

Then one of the Twin Towers collapsed as we watched in disbelief, still trying to describe it for our listeners.

Some other radio stations simulcast their sister all-news stations or broadcast audio from television. Others, with no other options, kept playing "the best mix of your favorite music," as if nothing unusual were going on at all.

It was as if we'd been preparing for this type of thing since we did our very first show. We were communicating what we knew for sure, what we were being told, and what we suspected, not because we were journalists or had been trained to report, but because we simply did what came naturally.

I still get chills when I hear the recordings of our show that morning. But I am proud of what we were all able to do, keeping everyone updated on what we could learn about the situation, naturally hypothesizing without causing panic. Proud of the entire staff and contributors, too, and even the listeners who contributed. Speedy, Don Juan, Roxanne, Jim Dunaway, Mark Prater, Mickey Dean. Proud but not especially pleased that even our speculation turned out to be mostly accurate.

During that horrible morning, Rick invited believers to "hit their knees" and ask for God's intervention. There would be other times over the years that we would be called upon to drop the jokes and fun and react to what was happening in the world, to events in our own lives.

But it would be about six and a half years after that awful September morning when we would face an even tougher opportunity to ad-lib our way through something tragic. That opportunity was, I strongly believe, the culmination of where the *Rick and Bubba Show* had been going all along.

We relied on our instincts when we did that September 11 show.

Another radio show Speedy and I would eventually be led to do required nothing short of divine guidance.

17 Satan's Miscalculation

I love that last verse in Psalm 31: "Be of good courage, and he shall strengthen your heart, all ye that hope in the Lord." That chapter talks about grief and relying on God when our hearts are breaking. It starts with the words, "In thee, O Lord, do I put my trust."

None of us know, though, if our faith is enough until it is tested, until something happens that we could never have anticipated. Nor can we imagine how it might eventually affect us. Us and so many others.

———

God blessed me—Rick—with five beautiful children. I suppose it was my idea to give each of them their own unique nicknames. Or it may have been that with all their names beginning with a "B," it gave us a way to pick one of them out to fuss at without calling the roll: "Brandi! Blake! Brooks! Brody! Bronner! Which one of you put the brownie in the DVD player?"

Bubba helped with our daughter's nickname. Because she was so good at sports, he suggested "Jo Jo Burgess" after champion ice skater Jo Jo Starbuck. It fit. And it stuck.

Blake, my oldest son, was (and still is . . . if I may brag a bit) also a good athlete. As of this writing, he's playing football collegiately for the Auburn Tigers in the mighty Southeastern Conference.

I know, I know. I'm living my dream through my son.

But like his dad, Blake has not always totally been into the game. That was obvious at a pressure-packed Little League game one time when he was up there on deck, ready to bat. The winning run stood on second base, in scoring position.

I couldn't resist a quick pep talk for my boy.

"Blake, all you need to do is get the ball out of the infield, and you win the game," I told him through the backstop fence. "Just connect with the ball and give your base runner a chance to score."

He was clearly not paying any attention to me. Instead he was staring idly up at the night sky, looking at something above the bugs and lights.

"Dad, is that the Big Dipper or the Little Dipper?"

He did connect and get the ball out of the infield, his team won the game, and—in reaction to the big, game-winning hit—he was forever-more nicknamed "Boomer."

Brooks is a big kid with a bigger heart. When he was still a toddler, he loved to grab other kids in Sunday school and hug them so hard they both ended up on the floor at the feet of their frustrated teacher. He once hugged Bubba's daughter, Katelyn, right through a table.

His nickname was obvious. "Big Love."

Brody's nickname was established from the time he first learned to crawl. He is constantly in motion, spinning, whirling, knocking over stuff, and creating mayhem, just like the cartoon character the Tasmanian Devil. So Brody will forever be known as "Taz."

Because they were so close in age, and shared so many of the same superheroes, Big Love and Taz also combined to wreak much more havoc than a couple of kids that age should have ever been able to manage. So we tagged them with a secondary nickname, "the Killer Bs."

Our youngest, Bronner, decided at age six months that bland and boring baby food was not for him. One day I got tired of trying to stuff pureed carrots into his mouth, only to have them end up in my lap and all over the kitchen wall. I reached over and pinched off a corner of a pone of cornbread and put it on his tray.

Bronner knew instinctively that this was, compared to the "orange putty" I'd been trying to force-feed him, some kind of real food. He grabbed the cornbread on his own, shoved it into his mouth, and pounded on his tray, demanding some more of that wonderful stuff.

That was a sign. He was immediately dubbed "Cornbread."

Parents know what I mean when I say that your children will bring out emotions in you that you didn't know you had. Emotions that range from the most intense anger to the most unbelievable pride. That's because we love them so much, even when they plug the cat's tail into the wall socket or scream bloody murder in a nice restaurant and refuse to hush because they want chocolate pudding instead of whatever dessert is on the menu. Or hijack a golf cart at a nice country club and crash it into an expensive SUV. (Yes, it actually happened.) Once you get over the "Thank God you are all right" feelings, then all those other emotions come raging through.

Parents merely look on and grin knowingly. You can read their lips.

"Payback," they say to each other, nodding. "Payback!"

Then they proceed to spoil their grandkids rotten, allowing them to get away with things that would have earned us the spanking of the century.

Only when we have children of our own do we truly appreciate our parents. I was blessed with a pair of great ones. People come up to me all the time and tell me that my dad literally changed their lives when they played football for him. As I have mentioned, he was a tough man, a demanding taskmaster, but every one of his players knew he cared about them, about their success, not just on the football field but in the much more important game of life.

Thinking back, I didn't realize it at the time, but my dad and mom loved me and supported me unconditionally. As a parent myself, I know how difficult that can be sometimes.

Being quick to discipline is the easy part of being a parent. Even worse are the many parents who do not really take much of a part in their children's lives because they are "too busy," too occupied with a job, trying to afford to buy the material things they think really matter.

Those are just ways to ignore the important—and more difficult—part of being mommas and daddies: loving our children unconditionally. Supporting them, even when their choices are not necessarily the ones we would make for them. Establishing boundaries and enforcing them. Making sure they know the right thing to do is not always the easiest thing to do. In fact, it rarely is.

That stuff is hard! But we have to accept the challenge, no matter how much work it is.

One of my favorite passages of Scripture is John 16:33. It says, "I have told you these things, so that in me you may have peace. In this world, you will have trouble. But take heart! I have overcome the world" (NIV).

Even now, after the things that have happened to my family, I still find so much comfort in that one short verse. I *do* take heart! It not only tells us; it *guarantees* us that we will have trouble in this life. And by trouble, I think Jesus is talking about misery, disappointment, sorrow, and pain, and a whole bunch of other bad things I could name but don't have to.

However, here is our Savior, reminding us that He has conquered the world and He is standing by, ready to help us overcome our own troubles. All we have to do is humble ourselves and allow Him to do so.

I believe this with all my heart. But when I wrote about this in one of our previous books, I had no idea how soon Sherri and I and the rest of our family would have to draw comfort from that concept.

In January 2008, Satan made a huge miscalculation.

It was me who was away from home this time, and Sherri was there with the boys. I was doing an event for Scott Dawson Ministries in Pigeon Forge, Tennessee. It was an intense group of powerful sessions, held simultaneously at three different venues around town. Those of us who were presenting were being hustled from one site to the other, speaking to a group while others were presenting elsewhere, for a total of six different presentations. It is such a wonderful event and always leads hundreds of young people to follow Christ. I was honored that Scott asked me to be there and to be a part of it.

I noticed when I was onstage that my cell phone kept vibrating like crazy. I checked the caller ID. It was my home number. I figured it was one of the kids calling me to tell me good night. They did that often. Finally, between sessions number four and five, I had a chance to return the call.

It was Sherri. She was distraught.

She had left the three boys downstairs in the family room for just a few minutes to take a shower. They were watching television, engrossed in a movie. But when she came back into the room, she noticed that Bronner was missing. The door to the outside was ajar. We still don't know if it was left unlocked or if he'd learned to unlock it, but somehow he'd managed to get it open and had gotten outside.

Sherri found him in our swimming pool. He was clinging to life when they transported him to the hospital, but she knew in her heart that God had called him home.

Satan, as he so often does, had struck a mighty blow.

Almost in a daze, I told everyone around me what had happened and asked them to pray. For Bronner. For Sherri. For Rick.

You have to believe me when I tell you this: despite the horror of hearing the news that my precious child had been taken from us, at that awful moment I instantly felt the power of God surround me, engulf me, as surely as if Christ had put His arms around me and pulled me close to Him.

I got in touch with Bill after some cell phone complications. He's the ultimate problem solver and was already busy trying to arrange for an airplane to get me home. I had driven up to Pigeon Forge from Birmingham, and it would take me the rest of the night to get back home. I'm sure Bill and the others were worried about my being alone for that long drive home, too.

I knew that Bronner's death was for a reason. God's reason. Everything I knew and believed about God and His promises to us absolutely screamed that. Whatever He does has a purpose. But in the back of my mind, I knew that this had to be more than just a test of Sherri's and my faith. It was an opportunity for something else, something bigger. I just didn't know at that grief-stricken moment what, exactly, it was.

However, once I was on the plane headed for Birmingham, one word kept coming to me over and over.

Perplexed.

As I prayed, it became just a little bit clearer. God wanted people to be perplexed by how Sherri and I would react to Bronner's loss. I still had no idea what, exactly, that meant.

When I later looked up the word *perplex*, it was defined as "to confuse with uncertainty or doubt." I still could not fathom how things might play out over the blur of days that stretched out ahead of us, or why God wanted people confused about and just plain doubting our family's faith.

The pilot of the plane loved Jesus and told me so. He promised he would get me home just as quickly as he could, and he did. I didn't know a little prop plane could get us from East Tennessee to Birmingham so fast. He let it eat!

As we flew, I looked out the window at the beautiful winter moon and the stars that are so bright and clear at that altitude on a cold night. I thought about it all some more and, like the stars, I suspected it would become more distinct for me—God would make it clear why this had happened and what I was supposed to do.

I knew there was a reason for this tragedy, for the suffering we would have to endure, and God would reveal that reason in His own good time.

It never occurred to me that the revelation would come to me at the funeral of my precious son.

18   God's Megaphone

As much as Rick and I love what we do, there are shows we hope we never have to do. We don't always feel as happy as we sound. There are days it's difficult to open that microphone and carry on.

Sometimes, though, the best things we do come at a time when it's the hardest to get it done. That's when we simply rely on our instincts and our Lord to carry us through.

═══

When Rick called us that cold, cold night, Betty answered the telephone. She was almost hysterical when I took the phone from her. A few minutes later, after having cell phone problems, Rick called back and I answered. He was amazingly calm.

"Bronner is gone, Bill," he told me. "I'm not worried about him. I know where he is. But Sherri needs you guys. I need you too. Can you help me get home?"

I am a "fixer," and to tell the truth, I'm glad I had this chore to do. It gave me a chance to do something to help. Something besides just hitting my knees and praying.

I remember all the chaos, the continual ringing of my cell phone, as we raced for the hospital to be with Sherri. We prayed all the way that there had been a mistake, that the little fellow had made it after all. Somehow, in the midst of it all, some other folks and I worked on rounding up a couple of pilots and an airplane to run to Knoxville and pick up Rick and get him back to Birmingham.

When he walked from the plane to where I waited for him at the airport, I didn't know what to say or do. I just gave him a bear hug.

Once we got to the hospital, we talked about a lot of things. Rick mentioned that he felt Romans 8 was coming alive. In the Bible, Romans 8, verses 14 through 19 says,

> For as many as are led by the Spirit of God, these are sons of God. For ye received not the spirit of bondage again unto fear; but ye received the spirit of adoption, whereby we cry, Abba, Father. The Spirit itself beareth witness with our spirit, that we are children of God: and if children, then heirs; heirs of God, and joint-heirs with Christ; if so be that we suffer with him, that we may be also glorified together. For I reckon that the sufferings of this present time are not worthy to be compared with the glory which shall be

revealed in us. For the earnest expectation of the creation waiteth for the manifestation of the sons of God.

We suffer, but the reward awaits us.

Rick turned to me, looked me in the eye, and told me, "Bill, I think you and Speedy need to do the show Monday."

I confess I had not even thought about the show at that point. Once Rick mentioned it, though, I felt a chill in my gut.

"Rick, I don't know what we'll say," I replied.

"God will tell you. Bill, this is not a defeat. Like Jesus told the disciples, 'I will tell you what to say.'"

I love all of Rick's kids, but I felt a special connection with Bronner. I was there at the hospital the day he was born. That night, as Betty and I rode toward a different hospital where he now lay dead, I remembered what a wonderful, fun, and relaxed event that day of his birth was. Because Sherri's delivery was so easy and quick that time, none of the family had made it to the hospital yet. Rick and I had a running show going that day, enjoying the moment. I was the one who took pictures of Rick proudly holding his new son.

Now I was going to have to go on the radio two days after Bronner died and do a show. A show? How in the world would we be able to pull that off?

Speedy and I met with the program director and many other staff members at the station on Sunday afternoon and confirmed that we would be on the air the next day. We had already been interviewed by every television station in the area and had used that opportunity to witness, to talk about the strength the Burgess family was drawing from their faith, even in the wake of this tragic event. One reporter from Fox News wanted me to comment on swimming pool safety in the interview.

"Look, this ain't about pool safety," I told her. "This is about spiritual warfare."

She looked at me funny, but I think she knew what I was saying.

Speedy and I rerecorded all of Rick's live endorsement commercials, assuming the sponsors would understand if his voice was not on them for a few days. Then he and I assured the program director that doing the show was the right thing. I'm not certain that he was convinced. He had only worked with us for a short time and didn't know us that well yet.

"But what are you going to say?" he asked us.

"We'll just be ourselves," I told him, though I still hadn't a clue how we would address what had happened, or exactly what we would say. There was no doubt this would be the largest listening audience we had ever assembled. We definitely had to do a live show. I was also starting to get an inkling of what we might be able to accomplish that dark Monday. "We'll do it just like we did the 9/11 show," I told him.

"What about the next few days, though?"

I knew what he was asking. How long would the audience want this to go on? How long would they still want to hear about Bronner's death before things got back to "normal"?

"We'll know," I assured him. "We'll know how to handle it."

Then he asked the question I knew had been on his mind all along.

"Bill, do you think Rick will ever come back to the show? Do you think the show will ever get back to normal?"

I suspected—and quite correctly—that the show would never be quite the same again. It would be changed profoundly. But I also knew the character of Rick Burgess.

"He'll be back," I said. "He'll find his peace behind that microphone."

That was a tough few days for my family, too, but an amazing thing happened. Our daughter had already accepted Christ, but our son was still not sure and had many questions. That was especially true after God took someone he knew well, someone so young and innocent. At a family meeting, Hunter listened as we talked about Job and about bad things happening to good people. He asked again about heaven, about walking with Christ. Through Bronner's loss, Hunter found salvation.

As we lost one son—temporarily—we gained two for eternity. Praise Jesus!

I woke up even earlier than usual that Monday morning. Betty didn't have to kick me out of bed to shut off the alarm clock. As I cranked up the truck and started for the station, I felt completely at ease, a reassuring calm washing over me.

I deliberately took a long way to work, having church all by myself right there in the cab of my truck. I remembered a quote attributed to C. S. Lewis that says, "Pain and suffering are merely God's megaphone for a sleeping world."

That would be our show that morning: God's megaphone.

Speedy started the show as usual with the National Anthem. I briefly recapped for the audience exactly what had happened, straightforward and matter-of-factly. I knew many listeners considered themselves part of the "family" and wanted to know what had actually occurred the previous Saturday night. Rumors were going around that needed to be quashed, too, so I told it straight.

"It's a nightmare," I said. "It's like a truckload of bricks was dumped on us. We are hurting for Rick and his family."

The words seemed to come easier then as I remembered what Rick had said to me that awful night as we drove toward the hospital. I knew true friends of the show wanted to know about Rick and Sherri and were hurting for them, too.

"This gives us the chance to show that our faith that we demonstrate here on the show is not just window dressing. Rick wants you to know he's worried about all of you; he wants you to know that we should all be ready to put on our armor and be ready to battle against Satan. I'm proud of Rick, but I'm not surprised. He's strong and has risen to the occasion for Sherri and his family."

Speedy and I played some songs by friends like Christian singer Kevin Derryberry and others. I talked about Lazarus and how that story of rising from the dead—one of my favorites from the Bible—demonstrated the power Jesus has over death. Listeners could hear my voice crack as I recounted how Jesus rolled back the stone at the grave of Lazarus and demonstrated that he was alive, a foreshadowing of the eventual resurrection of Christ.

I am no minister or theologian, but the words poured out, and amazingly they made sense. It seemed perfectly natural. Rick had been right. God told me what to say and put the words in my mouth.

Listeners joined in the show, as they so often do, giving their own real and sincere testimony.

"Bubba, you and Rick have gotten so many of us through tough times with what you do every day. Now it's our turn to help you get through a terrible time. We are praying for you all."

"We feel like we are part of the family, too, and we are hurting."

"I was in Pigeon Forge Saturday, and I heard a young man talking about how Rick Burgess changed his life that day with what he said. He accepted Jesus. But you know what? That was before anybody knew what had happened. When we found out, thousands of teenagers were praying for Rick and Sherri. Thank you and Speedy for being there this morning. God is working through you."

"Heaven is a whole lot livelier this morning because 'Cornbread' is there!"

The effect of the show on the audience that day was nothing short of miraculous, not because of anything Speedy or I said, or any of the music we played. We would later hear stories about people who were listening while driving to work. They pulled over and prayed. People accepted Christ and began a walk with Him right there on the side of the freeway. Folks held prayer sessions in offices and factories that day. Others shared the gospel openly and unashamedly with family, friends, and coworkers for the very first time that day. All that was because of what had happened to Rick and Sherri.

Of course, Speedy and I had no idea it would happen this way. Like the 9/11 program, there are shows we hope we never have to do. Sometimes we forget the power of the platform the Lord has given us, but thankfully, we found out once again its mighty influence that Monday morning in January 2008.

God's megaphone woke up lots of folks that day!

19 Jesus, Take the Wheel

YouTube was invented the same year Bronner Burgess was born. A few years later, his dad's eulogy would be the most-watched video on YouTube for days on end.

Tell me God does not work from a big and wonderful schematic!

———

I knew Bubba and Speedy had the show handled. I never had a doubt. When I heard about the impact those broadcasts had—that Monday morning and the several days after—I was not one bit surprised. See, God had already told me it would happen.

I was still not sure I had my own next several days put together so solid, though. There would be a memorial service for Bronner at our church. Our church family had surrounded us, wrapped us up in love, and that was a wonderful comfort. Though a voice still whispered to me that this would be an opportunity for Bronner's life—and ultimately his death—to mean something more, I still wasn't sure where, when, or how.

Maybe it was the way Bubba and Speedy did the show and the hundreds, if not thousands, they had led to a closer walk with Christ that morning. Maybe that was it.

As we neared the time for the service, I spoke with our pastor, Danny Wood. He shared briefly with me the gist of the message he was planning to bring, and it was a fine one, clearly inspired by the Lord. He asked if I wanted to say something during the service, reminding me that I didn't have to. Nobody expected it. They would understand.

"I think I'll just get up and say a few words, thank everyone for all they've done," I told him.

Well, Brother Danny never got the chance to deliver that inspired message he was planning.

The fatigue and emotion of the past few days had drained me, and I felt weak, washed out. Truthfully, I just wanted to get through the memorial, thank everybody, and go home.

When I walked into the sanctuary, however, I saw the pictures of Cornbread being projected on the big screens. Suddenly I felt a supernatural strength take hold of me. It had to be the same feeling that grabs people when they are blessed with amazing strength to lift a car off a person or run incredibly fast to help somebody they love who is in trouble.

"I will provide the words."

The voice in my head was as clear and distinct as those of the church family who shook my hand, hugged us, and told us they were praying for God to give us strength. Like the words of the country song, Jesus was about to take the wheel.

When I got up on that stage, I was a ventriloquist's dummy. I sat on God's knee, and He spoke through me.

Look, I am a performer. I love being in the spotlight, in front of a crowd. I craved it when I was a kid in Cheaha Acres, playing entertainer. I am more comfortable in front of thousands of folks or on a microphone speaking to millions than I am in a room with two or three people.

But it wasn't Rick Burgess talking to the crowd and cameras that day. I'm just not that articulate. It wasn't Bronner's earthly father delivering that message.

It was Bronner's and my heavenly Father speaking through me. I even said so during the message.

"An earthly father could not get up here and speak like this today. My heavenly Father can," I told the crowd.

When I watch the YouTube video of my presentation, the first thing I notice is how often I wander over to the middle of the stage during the message and lean on the centerpiece that stands in front of the altar. I wasn't even aware I was doing that.

That centerpiece is a cross.

If you'd like to watch the presentation, it's on YouTube.com. Just type "William Bronner Burgess" in the search box.

Much later, when I saw another video—the video we ultimately used for a tribute to Bronner on one of his birthdays and that also received thousands more views on YouTube—I noticed something in one of the clips for the first time. There was a moving scene in the video that showed Sherri sitting in a pew, watching me speak. She was holding up her hand, clearly reaching up for God's hand. I believe she will verify that He offered it to her during that service, as well as before and afterward. His hand and a loving, comforting embrace from the Great Comforter.

I talked that day about how my flesh, in the face of this tragedy, yearned to just stop living, to go on to the next world. That, of course, would be the natural reaction for any earthly father who had just lost his son. However, Jesus defeated death, a death He did not have to suffer but went through it anyway because He loved us so much. In so doing, Jesus gave every single one of us a clear choice. We can make the decision to ignore that wonderful sacrifice and simply die. Many do, every day. On the other hand, we can make the decision to live for Him.

Then, how do we endure a loss like Sherri and I had just suffered? Where do we turn? I talked about John 14, which contains that very straightforward promise: "Let not your heart be troubled . . . I will not leave you comfortless: I will come to you." The Great Comforter.

And somehow I remembered those wonderful words from John 16:22: "And ye now therefore have sorrow: but I will see you again, and your heart shall rejoice, and your joy no man taketh from you." That was Jesus, promising the disciples that even though He would go away from them—that He would die, as we know death to be—He would still meet them again, they would still see Him again one day. Just as Sherri and I know with certainty that we will see Bronner again.

You think those words from the Bible weren't powerful for my family and me during that time? That they didn't sustain us when we were hurting the most?

I know now that the message God spoke through me at Bronner's memorial service was aimed as much at me as it was at the thousands who sat there in that sanctuary, watching and listening. And for the millions more who would later watch it on YouTube and through other venues.

In the crowd that day were ministers, listeners of the show, family, friends, and even the governor of the state of Alabama. There were people who were true believers, those who were definitely not, and those who were on the fence about their own salvation. Many in the sanctuary that day disagreed theologically with almost everything I preached about. But thank God, hearts were touched across the board.

Oh, the loss of our little boy was traumatic. Even in our faith, there is pain. God hurt, too, when Jesus suffered that awful death on the cross. We wept for our son. So did He. It still hurts. We still miss Cornbread.

But even now, years later, I hear regularly from people who found Christ—who are still doing so—precisely because of the loss of our precious little boy. People who were at the conference that night, where hundreds came to Christ, people who heard Bubba and Speedy on those inspired shows that week on the radio, and those who saw the YouTube videos or the news broadcasts. People who were perplexed about how we would handle such a cruel loss in the face of the faith we had so strongly and publicly professed.

That "little evangelist"—as God described William Bronner

Burgess through my words—led untold numbers to Christ, many of whom only knew us through the radio show or who had only heard about us after that terrible night. They saw God working through my family and through those precious, unplanned hours on the radio show with Bill and Speedy.

Maybe it didn't happen at that moment. Maybe it took them days or weeks or years. Maybe they're still looking and will find it later. Maybe the words I am writing now, the retelling of this story, will be what it takes. I hope they will come to know the Lord before it's too late. How many souls were saved or will be saved or lives altered we will never know, at least not in this life. Maybe God will share the numbers with me when I join Him in heaven.

Now do you see why I am convinced that Jesus took the wheel that day and spoke through this fat deejay?

Satan picked on the wrong bunch of believers. God allowed it to happen, and in so doing, He used the platform with which He blessed Bubba and me.

Through us, so very many came to know Him and His precious Son, Jesus. Bronner did not die in vain any more than our precious Jesus Christ did.

20   Who We Are

We love it when either of us is out somewhere and a fan rec-
ognizes us and screams, "Rick and Bubba!" First, we're just
thankful we have fans. For a couple of fat guys with syrupy
Southern accents to accomplish that on a medium like radio
is miraculous enough. Secondly, it is a thrill that people feel
like they know us well enough to come right up and talk with
us as if we are supposed to know them too.

It's great, too, that they see us as inseparable. Either
one of us is still "Rick and Bubba." We've been in this "marriage" for a long time now, and we've never had a fight or
threatened a breakup.

You think God has some reason that He wants us to stay
together, or what?

So that is how we became Rick and Bubba. Our show has changed a whole bunch since we started reading Shakespeare with a Southern accent on the Q in Gadsden, Alabama. Since we started imitating characters who had made cameo appearances in our real lives, like Dippin' Dan, with his lip full of snuff; Carwash Joe, the world's worst boss; or Dickie Nadmire, who simply cannot understand the world as it is and stays quite irritable with everybody he encounters in it.

It is a fact that we—Rick and Bubba—are not the same as we were when we were twenty-five years old. If the show is about us and everything that goes on around us, it has to evolve and reflect the changes in our lives.

Rick and Bubba have met many celebs over the years. The fat boys pictured here with Charles Barkley at a charity golf tourney

We're convinced that we're finally comfortable with who we are. When I—Rick—listen to tapes of the show in the early days, I cringe when I hear that fake deejay voice I used on the air. And when I—Bubba—realize how we avoided talking about so many things that were important to us . . . religion, politics, hunting . . . to concentrate on what the stations wanted us to talk about, I feel bad about all the precious time and radio waves we wasted.

Funny, but the more the show evolved, the bigger and more loyal the listening audience became. Hey! And we will admit, too, that the bigger the show grew, the more financially successful we were. The more the broadcast consultant goobs and research-loving program directors railed about how we had to toe the format line, the more the people appreciated what we were doing. The Lord has blessed us far beyond anything either of us could have ever imagined when we were doing radio remotes and missing important events in our lives, or struggling, trying to keep a little Christian-music radio station out of bankruptcy.

Do not think for a minute that we don't know that God can take it all away from us tomorrow. If it serves His purpose, He will.

We still love what we do for a living, and almost certainly more than ever. Rick still hates to get up in the morning, and sometimes Bubba would much rather be hunting deer at the Bubbarosa or charging for the net at center court in a good game of tennis. But we believe strongly that the Rick and Bubba Army could tell in a second if we were faking it, phoning it in, and we owe them far too much to ever do that.

We also have some great folks who work with us, and we owe it

217

to them to always do our best, too. They certainly do, every single day.

I—Rick—am blessed to still have both my parents. Jacksonville State University recently honored my dad by naming the football field at the school after him. That was a wonderful way of recognizing all the hard work he put into his time there. You think he won't let me know it if he thinks I'm doggin' it on the show?

And I—Bubba—still have Mom. A woman who once plowed a mule to help feed her family would never allow me to goof off.

If it's God's plan, we'll put on station T-shirts again, crank up the Funmobile (hoping we left it parked in a place where we would not have to rely on reverse gear to get going), and go hand out free hot dogs and balloons for the kids at some shopping center remote broadcast.

Those same radio "experts" continue to tell us that we need more guests on the show, more comedians and authors and movie stars and less Christian music and Sunday school and what the Busseys and Burgesses or Speedy or Greg or the interns did over the weekend. They advise us that we shouldn't talk so much about church, food, hunting, fishing, our kids, or tennis. That we should go back to more comedy bits, like "Good Old Boy Theater." (Of course, some of those "experts" were the same ones who thought Bubba reading quotes from the works of the Bard on the air was the worst radio they had ever heard!)

How we became "big" is simple. And we're not talking about all those fried chicken livers or double cheeseburgers or free food we have gobbled up over the years.

We allowed God to guide us. We took what He gave us and we ran with it. As long as we continue to do that, He will continue to bless us. As I—Rick—said at Bronner's memorial, God never promised that things would always be easy. On the contrary, we know we have bad things to dread, setbacks and disappointments, sickness and death.

However, we also know that we will remain strong in the face of all that. We are both certain that we will not be easily defeated so long as we work hard and the Holy Spirit, the Great Comforter, is with us.

Oh, it is such a wonderful thing to know with certainty that He will be at our side, as long as we are with Him.

That, when you get right down to it, is how "we be big."

The End

Acknowledgments

We would like to thank first and foremost Almighty God for the mercy and grace He has had on all of our lives. Without Him all hope is lost and our desire to do this show would be meaningless.

God has blessed us with wives that have supported us and carried us through so much of this journey. Thanks to our wives for always keeping us humble and reminding us of who we really are and why we do the show.

Thanks to our children who have had to deal with what it's like to grow up in front of an audience and for providing us with so much radio gold. For teaching us so much about the love our heavenly Father has for us.

Thanks to our Moms and Dads for their never ending influence on everything we do.

Thanks to the staff who keep the RICK AND BUBBA train moving forward: Calvin "speedy" Wilburn, "THE REAL" Greg Burgess, Michael "Helmsey" Helms, and Chris "Eddie Van" Adler.

Thanks to COX Broadcasting for being such a wonderful broadcast partner and for giving us the freedom to do the show we feel lead to do.

Thanks to Syndicated Solutions for continuing to move the chains and take this show across the nation.

Thanks to all our interns past, present, and future.

Thanks to Zeekee Interactive for all your work on rickandbubba .com.

Thanks to David Sanford, who gave up all his credibility by becoming our literary agent.

Thanks to Rick and Bubba contributors: James Spann, Ken "bones" Hearns, Mark Gentle, Don Yessick, and Erik Hastings.

Thanks to Thomas Nelson for believing we could actually produce books that anyone would read.

Thanks to Don Keith for lowering himself to this project and telling our story.

Thanks to all of our guests over the years. Sorry for not letting you talk as much as you might have hoped.

Last but not least, Thank *you*, for buying this book and for being part of the blessing that God continues to provide through you and your support of the show. You have been used by God to make so many of our dreams come true.

Rick and Bubba

I would like to thank Rick and Bill for trusting me enough to allow me to help them tell their story. They suspected that, as a former broadcaster who knew many of the people mentioned here, an amateur radio operator (N4KC), a friend, and a neighbor, I would "get it." I hope they still feel that way! I'd also like to acknowledge all my own listeners and readers down through the years. Without them, we would all be talking to the wall. And finally, thank you to Charlene, my wife of forty-three years, who still tolerates my obsession for telling stories to perfect strangers.

Don Keith